Contents

(barcode) **W9-BRE-519**

Study Skills: Listening

Quiz   p. 7

Section 1   p. 7
Skills: prediction, recognizing repetition and avoiding distracters, listening for numbers and letters
Question types: multiple choice, completing notes

Section 2   p. 11
Skills: using key words for prediction, eliminating wrong answers, completing a summary
Question types: multiple choice, summary completion, sentence completion

Section 3   p. 13
Skills: listening for specific speakers, listening for specific information / short answers, completing a table, classifying, spelling
Question types: completing a table, short answers, classifying

Section 4   p. 16
Skills: labelling a diagram with numbered parts, labelling a flow chart, sentence completion, listening for signpost words
Question types: sentence completion, labelling a diagram with numbered parts, labelling a flow chart

Study Skills: Reading

Quiz   p. 19

Reading Passages 1 and 2   p. 19
Skills: skimming for gist, matching headings to paragraphs / pictures, charts and diagrams, multiple choice, guessing meaning from context
Question types: matching headings to paragraphs, completing charts, tables and diagrams, multiple choice

Reading Passages 3 and 4   p. 26
Skills: skimming for gist, scanning to find information quickly, short answer questions, understanding paraphrasing, *T/F/NG* and *Y/N/NG*, recognizing opinion
Question types: short answers, *yes, no, not given*, classifying, multiple choice

Reading Passages 5 and 6   p. 33
Skills: skimming for gist, summary completion, guessing meaning from context, note completion, understanding paraphrasing and sentence completion
Question types: summary completion, sentence completion, note completion

Study Skills: Writing

Quiz p. 37

Writing Task 1 p. 37
Understanding data
Language focus: Expressing figures and quantities
The opening statement
Language focus: Describing change over a period of time
Selecting and grouping key information
Language focus: Expressing comparison and contrast
Describing a process

Writing Task 2 p. 47
Understanding the instructions and the question
Understanding the topic and the task
Brainstorming and planning
The introduction
The main body
• Paragraphs and topic sentences
• Linking words
Conclusion
Further practice

Study Skills: Speaking

Quiz p. 54

Part 1 p. 54
Talking about familiar topics
Giving a good answer
Identifying strengths and weaknesses

Part 2 p. 56
Planning your answer
Giving extra information
Identifying strengths and weaknesses
Follow-up questions

Part 3 p. 57
Expanding answers
Linking ideas

Practice test p. 59

Answer key p. 71

Recording scripts p. 87

Introduction

Welcome to IELTS Foundation Study Skills. This is a different kind of exam practice book. As well as providing you with exam practice materials, this book will:
- Familiarize you with the different question types you will find in IELTS and give you guided practice in each of them.
- Help you to develop the skills you need to be successful.

There are four parts, corresponding to the four IELTS modules. Each part begins with *skills development*. In these sections you will develop your skills through focused exercises, with detailed guidance given in the key to each question. Next, in the *skills practice* sections, you can put what you have learnt into practice. Finally, the book contains a complete *Practice test*.

As IELTS Foundation is aimed at students starting at around 4–5.5, some of the reading and listening texts are shorter or the questions are a little easier than you would find in IELTS, especially towards the beginning. Essential vocabulary is given in a glossary. This will support you as you gradually develop your skills and improve your IELTS score.

For Writing and Speaking both model answers and sample student answers are given, so that you can start to evaluate your own work. Useful language is also provided.

The book is intended to be used for self study, but could also form the basis of a short intensive IELTS preparation course.

The IELTS Exam

IELTS, or the International English Language Testing System, is an exam designed to assess your level of English, on a scale from 1-9. The score you need will depend upon the course and the university you want to study at, but many students find they need to get an overall band score of 6.

Each section is weighted equally, but it is possible to get half band scores for the Reading and Listening modules (eg 5.5, or 6.5), but only whole number bands (eg 5, 6, 7 etc) for Speaking and Writing. Overall, therefore, you may get a half band score.

Band 9 – Expert User
Has fully operational command of the language: appropriate, accurate and fluent with complete understanding.

Band 8 – Very Good User
Has fully operational command of the language with only occasional unsystematic inaccuracies and inappropriacies. Misunderstandings may occur in unfamiliar situations. Handles complex detailed argumentation well.

Band 7 – Good User
Has operational command of the language, though with occasional inaccuracies, inappropriacies and misunderstandings in some situations. Generally handles complex language well and understands detailed reasoning.

Band 6 – Competent User
Has generally effective command of the language despite some inaccuracies, inappropriacies and misunderstandings. Can use and understand fairly complex language, particularly in familiar situations.

Band 5 – Modest User
Has partial command of the language, coping with overall meaning in most situations, though is likely to make many mistakes. Should be able to handle basic communication in own field.

Band 4 – Limited User
Basic competence is limited to familiar situations. Has frequent problems in understanding and expression. Is not able to use complex language.

Band 3 – Extremely Limited User
Conveys and understands only general meaning in very familiar situations. Frequent breakdowns in communication can occur.

Band 2 – Intermittent User
No real communication is possible except for the most basic information using isolated words or short formulae in familiar situations and to meet immediate needs. Has great difficulty in understanding spoken and written English.

Band 1 – Non User
Essentially has no ability to use the language beyond possibly a few isolated words.

Band 0 – Did not attempt the test
No assessable information provided.

A summary of each module is outlined below:

Listening

The Listening takes about 40 minutes and each section gets progressively more difficult.

Part	Number of speakers	Number of questions	Situation	Example
1	2	10	social/ general	Conversation between a student and a landlord
2	1	10	social/ general	Welcoming talk for a group of new students
3	2-4	10	academic	students in a seminar discussion
4	1	10	academic	a university lecture

Question Types: multiple choice, completing notes or sentences, completing or labelling diagrams, charts or tables, classifying, matching and writing short answers.

Exam Tips: You will only hear each section ONCE. However, there is time to look briefly at the questions before each part is played. During the exam, you should write on the question paper, and at the end you will have 10 minutes to transfer answers to the answer sheet. It is important to do this carefully, and check grammar and spelling, as mistakes will lose marks.

Academic Reading

The Reading lasts one hour and there are three reading texts, of increasing difficulty, taken from newspapers, magazines, books and journals. The topics are of general interest, so learners do not have to be experts in the subject area to understand them.

Question Types: multiple choice, choosing *true/ false/ not given*, or *yes/ no/ not given*, identifying the view of the writer, completing sentences or notes, completing or labelling diagrams, charts or tables, classifying, matching, choosing paragraph headings and writing short answers. There are 40 questions in total.

Exam Tips: As with the listening module, answers are written on an answer sheet, but *no extra time is given for this*. It is important that you practise managing your time (20 minutes for each section) so that you can complete the whole module within the hour by reading quickly and efficiently.

Academic Writing

There are two tasks in this module and it lasts 1 hour.

Task	Time	Number of words	Description of task
1	20 minutes	At least 150 words	Describe, compare and contrast information in diagrams, charts or tables, *or* describe the stages of a process, *or* explain how something works
2	40 minutes	At least 250 words	Give solutions to a problem, *or* present arguments in favour and against an opinion, *or* give and justify an opinion.

Assessment: In order to do well in Task 1, it is important to answer the question clearly, and organize your answer well. This may include grouping data appropriately and describing trends, rather than detailing every piece of information given. Your answer also needs to be accurate and include a good range of vocabulary.

In Task 2 slightly different assessment criteria are used. Here you need to ensure that you answer the question and include a clear and logical argument, giving evidence or examples where appropriate. Your answer also needs to be well organized and have a variety of vocabulary and grammatical structures used accurately.

Exam Tips: It is important to keep to the timings, as Task 2 is longer, and carries slightly more weight than Task 1. It is also important to keep to the word limits, as writing less than the number of words stated is likely to result in a lower score.

Speaking

The Speaking module takes between 11 and 14 minutes and is an oral interview between the learner and an examiner. It will be recorded on audio tape.

Part	Time	Description
1	4-5 minutes	General questions about home, family, studies, etc.
2	3-4 minutes	You are given a card with a topic and 3-4 prompt questions on it. You have 1 minute to prepare, and then have to speak for 1-2 minutes on that topic. At the end, the examiner may ask you a question.
3	4-5 minutes	Further discussion questions relating to the subject in part 2. This section requires you to give opinions, speculate and express reasons.

Assessment: Assessment is based on your fluency, the range, and accuracy of the vocabulary and grammatical structures you use, and your pronunciation.

Exam Tips: Try to relax during the exam, and give more extended responses to questions rather than just 'yes' or 'no' to gain higher marks. You can prepare for this module, for example, by practising speaking for 1-2 minutes on different topics. However, don't memorize long speeches as examiners can usually spot this, and will ask you to talk about something else.

Study Skills: Listening

The Listening module is the first part of the IELTS exam. Do this quiz to see how much you know about it.

Quiz

1 How long is the Listening module in total?
   A about 30 minutes   B about 40 minutes
   C about 50 minutes
2 How many sections are there?
   A 4   B 5   C 6
3 How many questions are there in total?
   A 25   B 30   C 40
4 The first part of the Listening module is the easiest and the last part is the most difficult. True or false?
5 Each section is worth the same number of marks. True or false?
6 There are four situation types in the Listening module. Match the examples with a situation type (A–D). Then number the situation types (A–D) in the order you will hear them.

Adam telephones a restaurant to book a table for a party.
Professor Jones lectures on climate change.
Steve, Mary and Sarah discuss their assignment on water pollution.

Mr Green gives a talk on how to open a bank account in the UK.

❏ A a monologue (one person speaking) in a university situation, eg a lecture
❏ B a monologue relating to social needs, eg a speech about arrangements for meals at a conference
❏ C a dialogue (two people talking together) relating to social needs, eg a conversation about travel needs
❏ D up to four people talking together in an academic situation, eg a conversation between a tutor and a student about an assignment

7 How many times do you hear each section?
8 Do you have time to read the questions before you listen?
9 Where should you write your answers?
10 You will lose marks for incorrect spelling. True or false?

Section 1

Remember
Read the **instructions** carefully so that you know what to do.
Read the **questions** carefully and predict what you will hear. Think about **who** is talking, **where** they are and **what** the topic is. In the exam you will only have a short time for this, so do it as quickly as possible.

Skills development

Prediction

Listening module section 1: Exam information
Number of people: two (a dialogue)
Context: conversation about social needs
Example situation: a student applying for a parking permit or someone reporting a stolen bag

1 Read the questions. Think about:

- who is talking
- what they are talking about
- any other useful information

1 How long has Keiko been at the college?
   A a day
   B a few days
   C a couple of weeks

2 The main building
   A has three floors.
   B is by a lake.
   C has a glass front.

3 Which door should she take for the accommodation office?
   A the first on the left
   B the second on the right
   C the second on the left

2 01 Listen and answer the questions.

Recognizing repetition and avoiding distracters

1 Read the recording script below. Which information is repeated?

Stephan: … when you get inside, go straight down the corridor, to the far end, and turn left. You'll see three doors on your left – accommodation is the middle one.
Keiko: So, I go along the corridor, turn left, and it's the second door on the left?
Stephan: That's right!

2 Look again at question 3. Why might someone choose B?

Completing notes

When completing notes, you will be given a word limit. You can write what you hear, but you might have to change the order of the words for the answer to make sense.

1 Rewrite these sentences. Write **NO MORE THAN THREE WORDS** for each answer. Check your answers are grammatically correct.

1 When you choose a university course, think about it carefully. It's a really important decision.
You need to ......*decide carefully*...... before you choose a university course.

2 You might like to study near to your home town, or to go further afield.
It is usually possible to study ......*in home town*...... or in another town or city.

3 The number of students who choose to study overseas is increasing very rapidly.
There has been a rapid rise in the number of students wanting to
......*study abroad*......

2 Keiko made some notes about the accommodation available through the college. Read the notes and predict the kind of information you need to listen for.

3 02 Listen and complete Keiko's notes. Write **NO MORE THAN THREE WORDS** for each answer.

4 Check your answers on page 71.

Three types of accommodation available:
- *Home stay*
  Cost of home stay: (1) $120 ....
  per week with meals
- *(2) ......college hall of resid......*
- *Private lets*
  College makes sure flats are
  (3) ......3 to 4 students......
  reasonably

First name: Keiko

Surname: (4) ....

Nationality: (5) ....

Address: The Sunrise Guest House

(6) ....

Phone number: (7) ....

email address: keiko@hotmail.com

5 🔲 03 Listen to the final part of the conversation between Keiko and the Accommodation Officer and complete the form.

Remember
All answers must be spelt and punctuated correctly.

Remember
Names of people and places always begin with capital letters. You will lose marks if you don't include them.

Listening for numbers and letters

1 🔲 04 How do you say these numbers in English? Listen and check your answers.

15   50   162   £3.25   47%   0.54   12,651

2 🔲 05 How do you say these letters in English? Listen and check your answers.

U   Y   L   O   G   X   I   P
Z   W   H   A   Q   R   E   B

3 🔲 06 How do you say these punctuation marks in English? Listen and check your answers.

1 **/**

2 **-**

3 **:**

4 **;**

5 **.** (in web addresses)

4 🔲 07 Listen and complete the notes with the appropriate words or numbers.

1   The man's name is ....

2   The answer is ....

3   The address is ....

4   Everest is ....high .

5   His name is ....

6   The address is ....

7   Her test score was ....

8   His favourite author is ....

9   The phone number is ....

10   The reference number is ....

11   The woman's name is ....

12   The address is ....

13   The web address is ....

14   The man wants to make an appointment with ....

15   The registration number is ....

Skills practice

Questions 1 and 2

🎞️ 08 For questions 1 and 2, listen and choose the correct answer.

1   How many people will be at Dan's party?
   A   10
   B   8
   C   18
   D   24

2   Which date does Dan book the party for?
   A   15th April
   B   16th March
   C   8th April
   D   16th April

Questions 3–5

While he was on the phone, Dan made some notes. For questions 3–6, listen and complete the notes. Write **NO MORE THAN THREE WORDS** for each answer.

For parties, the restaurant usually serves a (3) .... for a fixed price. There are three choices for each course, for example for starters there is prawn cocktail, soup or antipasto. At least one of the choices is (4) .... Also included in the price is (5) ....

Questions 6–9

For questions 6–9, listen and complete the booking form.

GIOVANNI'S
⤝‡‡⤞

Price per person: (6) £ ....

Deposit: (7) £ ....

Name: (8) ....

Phone number: (9) ....

Skills development

Listening module section 2: Exam information

Listening module section 2: Exam information
Number of people: one (a monologue)
Context: non-academic, social needs
Example situation: an informal talk on how to open a bank account

Using key words for prediction

1 Read questions **1–3** below and <u>underline</u> the important words. Can you think of synonyms for these words?

2 🔲 **09** Now answer questions **1–3**.

1 The programme
  A gives information about used car sales.
  B tells you the best way to buy a car.
  C tells you the most popular way to sell a car.
  D looks at different ways of buying a new car.

2 Which of the following reasons does the presenter give for someone wanting to buy a used car? Circle **THREE** letters **A–F**.
  A You are a new driver.
  B You have had an accident in your old car.
  C You don't have a lot of money.
  D Your old car is unreliable.
  E You want to learn to drive.
  F You need a bigger car.

3 One advantage of a dealer is
  A they have a lot of room to show you the cars.
  B they are cheap.
  C you have a legal right to return the car if something goes wrong.
  D they are honest.

Eliminating wrong answers

If you can eliminate even one or two wrong answers, you improve your chances of getting the right answer.

🔲 **09** Listen again and decide why the other answers to questions **1–3** above are wrong.

Completing a summary

1 Read this summary. For each gap, predict:
- the type of word missing (eg noun / verb / adjective)
- the kind of information it is asking for (use the context to help you)

A (1) .... way to buy a car is privately. Usually this is done by looking through the (2) .... and contacting the person selling the car directly. The (3) .... is that you will not get a warranty. If you are not knowledgeable about cars, you should have the car checked (4) .... You could also buy a car at auction. This could be very risky as you won't have (5) .... to inspect it properly before you buy it.

2 🔲 **10** Listen and complete the summary.

Remember
- The order of the questions follows the recording, so you can answer them in order.
- Think of synonyms or other ways of saying the important words.
- In a multiple-choice question you may have to choose two or more answers.

Remember
- Contractions such as *he's* count as two words.

Skills practice

Questions 1 and 2

🔲 11 Read through questions **1–3** and then listen and circle the appropriate letter.

1 What is Jenny Arnold's job?
   A Health and Safety Officer
   B Sports Coach
   C Health and Fitness Officer
   D Travel Agent

2 The subject of the lecture is
   A travelling.
   B staying safe and healthy abroad.
   C drawing classes.
   D summer holidays.

Question 3

Circle **TWO** appropriate letters.

3 Where does Jenny Arnold say you can get information about vaccinations?
   A from a hospital
   B from your doctor
   C from the Internet
   D from your local nurse
   E from NHS Direct

Questions 4–6

Read through questions **4–6** and complete the summary. Write **NO MORE THAN THREE WORDS** for each answer.

It is important to buy some (4) .... before you leave, even though it may be (5) .... , especially if you plan to do adventure sports. It will make your holiday more relaxing if you know that you could always (6) .... safely.

Questions 7–9

Read through questions **7–9** and then complete the sentences. Write **NO MORE THAN THREE WORDS** for each answer.

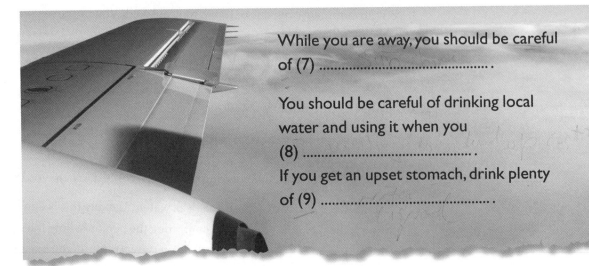

While you are away, you should be careful of (7) ....

You should be careful of drinking local water and using it when you (8) ....
If you get an upset stomach, drink plenty of (9) ....

Skills development

Listening for specific speakers

> **Listening module section 3: Exam information**
> Number of people: up to four people
> Context: education or training
> Example situations: a tutor and a student discussing an assignment, or a seminar situation with several students talking

🔲 12 Listen and answer the questions.

1 How many speakers are there in the conversation? How do you know?
2 What are their names?
3 How many times does each person speak?

Listening for specific information/short answers

1 Read the questions below and <u>underline</u> the key words. Which answer is a number? Which is a location or a situation? What *recent ecological problems* can you think of?

2 🔲 13 Listen and answer the questions. Write **NO MORE THAN THREE WORDS OR A NUMBER** for each answer.

1 Which **TWO** kinds of recent ecological problems does Anand mention?

  A ....

  B ....

2 What is the word limit for the assignment?

....

3 Where did Robert get his idea for a topic from?

....

Completing a table

1 Look at the table. Which questions ask you to identify types of pollution? Which answer is a date?

2 🔲 14 Listen and complete the table. Write **NO MORE THAN THREE WORDS** for each answer.

Pollution problem	Solution provided by	Completed
(1)	City Council	(2) ....
Boat traffic	(3)	next year
(4)	(5)	ongoing project

Classifying

For classification tasks, you have to match statements to one of three options. There may be more than one statement for each option.

1 Write the words in the box in the appropriate place in the table.

waste water
jet ski / motor boat fuel
rain and wind   crab
blown   marine life

Sea creatures	Stormy weather	Sewage	Emissions

2 Look at the question below and <u>underline</u> the key words.

3 🖭 15 For questions **1–4**:

if they refer to   Sewage   write   **S**
                   Boat traffic   write   **B**
                   Rubbish   write   **R**

> **Remember**
> You may have to use several options more than once.

1 Which kind of pollution can be used by sea creatures? ....
2 Which kind of pollution gets worse in stormy weather? ....
3 Which kind of pollution is increasing? ....
4 Which kind of pollution makes Sydney's population most upset? ....

Spelling

As in Section 2, sometimes words are spelt out for you, but often they are not. Even if the words are not spelt out, you must still spell them correctly.

1 🖭 16 Listen and complete the sentences.

1 The college is on the .... of an old castle.
2 The meeting will be held on ....
3 Please hand your essays in by next ....
4 We .... that you take the test in May.
5 The course is .... and highly beneficial.
6 .... rose dramatically in 2001.
7 I would .... you to do your homework.
8 He was a very successful ....
9 Different .... have different management systems.
10 He had a very .... career.
11 Studying abroad can help you become more ....
12 .... unwanted emails, or *spam*, is a growing problem.

2 Now check your answers on page 73.

3 Here is a list of words common in academic writing. Which **THREE** are spelt wrongly? Use your dictionary to check form and meaning.

accompany   consent
evident   percieved
suficient   specified

Skills practice

Questions 1–4

🔲 17 Complete the table. Write **NO MORE THAN THREE WORDS OR A NUMBER** for each answer.

	'A' Levels	Foundation Course
Length of course	2 years	1 year
Number of subjects studied	2–3	(1) ....
English language support given	often none	(2) .... per ....
Main type of assessment	exam(s)	(3) ....
Most popular with	(4)	overseas students

Questions 5–8

Write **NO MORE THAN THREE WORDS OR A NUMBER** for each answer.

5   What kind of English does Cathy study? ....

6   What does she say is different to her language? ....

7   Cathy studies the following modules:
   - economic theory
   - marketing strategies
   - ....

8   What does Brenda think about Cathy's course? ....

Questions 9–12

For questions **9–12**:
if they refer to   Millford University   write **M**
                    Ainsley University   write **A**
                    Parmouth University   write **P**

9   Which university has given Cathy a conditional offer? ....

10   Which university usually requires an IELTS score of 6.5? ....

11   Which university has a good reputation for Business Studies? ....

12   Which university is in a good location? ....

Skills development

Labelling a diagram with numbered parts

> **Listening module section 4: Exam information**
> Number of people: one (a monologue)
> Context: education or training
> Example situation: a lecture. The subject may be quite specific, but remember that you do not need any specialist knowledge to answer the questions.

1 Look at the following three diagrams.

1 Which one shows a plan or map?
2 Which one shows a process?
3 Which one shows an object?

Diagram 1

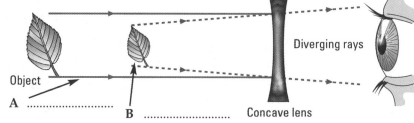

Object
A ....
B ....
Diverging rays
Concave lens

Diagram 2

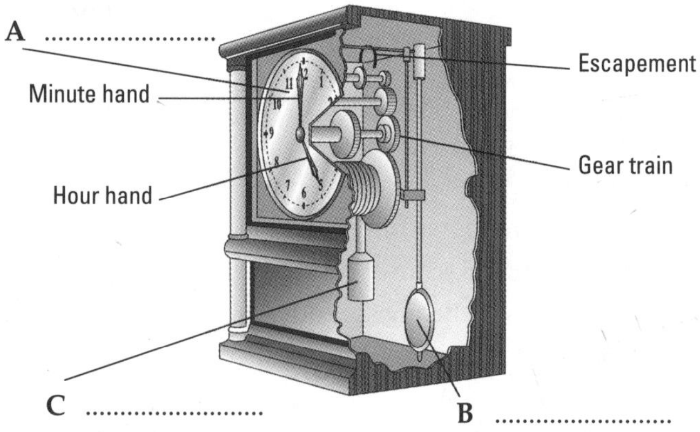

A ....
Minute hand
Hour hand
Escapement
Gear train
C ....
B ....

Diagram 3

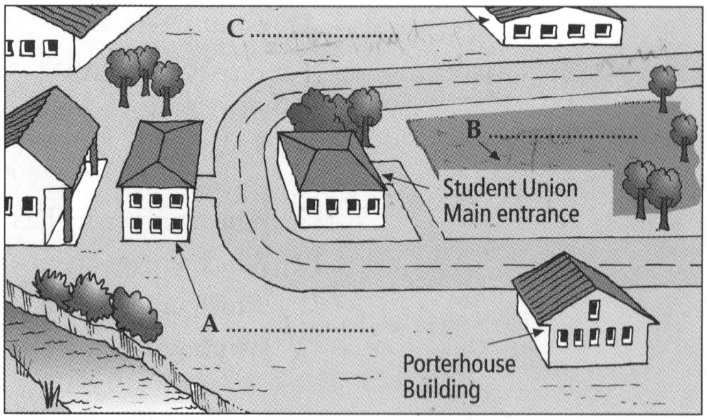

C ....
B ....
Student Union Main entrance
A ....
Porterhouse Building

2 🔲 18 Now listen and complete the labels on the diagrams.

3 Look at diagram 4. What does it show? Describe the positions of the numbered parts.

Remember
Study the diagram. Note what it shows and what positions things are in.

4 🔲 19
Listen and complete the labels. Write **NO MORE THAN THREE WORDS** for each answer.

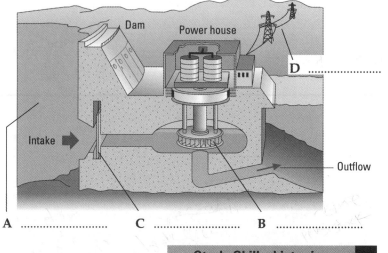

Dam
Power house
D ....
Intake
Outflow
A ....
C ....
B ....

Labelling a flow chart

1 Look at the flow chart below. Which answer is a number?

2 🔈 20 Complete the flow chart. Write **NO MORE THAN THREE WORDS OR A NUMBER** for each answer.

GENERATOR	❑ Create power
TRANSMISSION SUBSTATION Power at 1 .... volts	❑ Transforms electricity to high voltages
LOCAL POWER SUBSTATION Power at 7,200 volts	❑ Reduces voltage ❑ 2 .... ❑ Can turn off power if necessary
TRANSFORMER BOX/DRUM Power at 240 volts	❑ Lowers power to make it suitable for 3 .... service
CIRCUIT BREAKER/FUSE BOX	❑ Safety device to minimize 4 ....

Sentence completion

1 Is the information you need in the sentences below a noun, a verb or an adjective?

1 Two positive aspects of hydroelectricity are that it is .... and ....

2 One limiting factor of hydroelectricity is that it requires ....

2 🔈 21 Listen and answer the questions.

Listening for signpost words

Signpost words are words or phrases that tell a listener what the speaker is going to talk about next, eg *Right*, or *Anyway* indicate a change of subject and *for instance* indicates when the speaker is going to give an example.

Look at these extracts from the lecture on hydroelectricity. What do the <u>underlined</u> words indicate?

1 <u>I want to move on</u> today <u>to</u> a form of power that many would argue is far superior.
   A contrasting information
   B introducing a new topic
   C summing up

Remember
- You may be able to use words from the text, or you may need to change the form of the words, eg *reliable flow of water* (= four words), change to *reliable water flow* (= three words).
- You don't always need to

---

2 Right, <u>as you can see</u>, under the dam there is a control gate …
   A introducing a new topic
   B drawing attention to a visual
   C emphasising a point

3 <u>As we've said</u>, the power leaves the generator and enters …
   A recapping or reviewing information
   B summing up
   C adding extra information

Skills practice

Questions 1–4

22 Complete the sentences below. Write **NO MORE THAN THREE WORDS OR A NUMBER** for each answer.

1 Oil formation began between 10 million and .... years ago.

2 Dead plankton sank to the sea bed to mix with the ....

3 Layers of sediment put pressure and .... on the source rock.

4 Oil collects in porous rock, eg ....

Questions 5–7

Complete the diagram below. Write **NO MORE THAN THREE WORDS** for each answer.

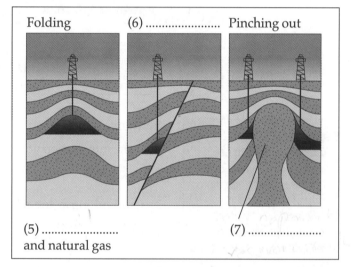

Folding   (6) ....   Pinching out

(5) .... and natural gas   (7) ....

Questions 8–12

Complete the flow chart using **NO MORE THAN THREE WORDS** for each answer.

Initial stages	Preparation for drilling	Drilling
Legal issues are settled.	Land is cleared and levelled. (8) .... may be built. A well is dug or a source of local (9) .... is found. Large, plastic-lined hole called a (10) .... is made. A *cellar* is dug at the site of (11)	Main hole begun with smaller drill. (12) Main rig is ....

Study Skills: Reading

How much do you know about the IELTS Academic Reading module?

Do the quiz below to find out.

1 How long is the Academic Reading module?
   A 90 minutes   **B** 60 minutes
   C 11–14 minutes

2 How many reading passages are there?
   A one   **B** four   **C** three

3 How many questions are there in total?
   A 35   **B** 40   **C** 55

4 Where can the reading passages come from?
   Tick any that you think are true.
   A magazines   ❏
   B newspapers   ❏
   C journals   ❏
   D letters   ❏
   E books   ❏
   F advertisements ❏

5 There is extra time for transferring your answers to the answer sheet at the end of the exam.
   True or false?

6 Texts and tasks are easier at the beginning of the exam than at the end.
   True or false?

7 All the questions are multiple choice.
   True or false?

8 At least one text contains detailed, logical argument.
   True or false?

In this section you will be looking at the skills you need to do well in the IELTS Academic Reading module and practising different question types.

Reading Passages 1 and 2

Remember
• Read the first sentence of each paragraph. This is usually the topic sentence, or the sentence that introduces the main topic of the paragraph.
• Don't worry if you don't know all the vocabulary. It may not be necessary in order to answer the questions.

Skills development

Skimming for gist

Read through the passage quickly to gain a general idea of the content. This will help when you come to look at the text in more detail, and is worth doing even when under pressure of time in the exam.

Read Reading Passage 1 in no more than three minutes and decide on the best general heading.

> **List of headings**
>   i What is skin cancer?
> ii Fun in the sun
> iii How to treat skin cancer
> iv How to protect yourself from skin cancer

A Many people enjoy sunbathing, but it is important to be aware of the risks of lying in the sun. Every year in the UK, there are more than 4,000 new cases of melanoma which is the most dangerous form of skin cancer. Up to 40 per cent of sufferers from melanoma will die. However, with the right precautions, it is possible to enjoy the sun and still stay safe.

B Sunshine contains three different bands of ultraviolet radiation: UVA, UVB and UVC. Although UVC is the most dangerous, because it is a shorter-wavelength radiation than UVA and UVB, it is screened out by the Earth's ozone layer. UVA used to be thought less dangerous than UVB, but it is now known that both bands can cause skin cancer. It is UVB which causes sunburn. However, both UVA and UVB can age the skin prematurely.

C Levels of UV rays can vary. A two-week holiday in the Mediterranean will expose you to the same amount of sun as you would get in a year in Britain. Short periods of intense exposure to the sun are thought to be more risky than regular daily exposure, particularly if you have fairer skin. However, even if you have darker skin tones you will burn eventually. You can find out the daily UV rate by watching the solar UV index which has recently been introduced on national weather forecasts across Europe.

D People haven't really been using sunbeds long enough to be sure of their full effects, but studies indicate that there may well be a potential risk of skin cancer. Because sunbeds use only UVA, you won't get sunburnt. However, this enables you to expose yourself to huge amounts of UVA, something you would not do at the beach where the prospect of getting sunburnt would limit your exposure. Sunbeds will also certainly contribute to your skin ageing more quickly.

E The ideal sunscreen to use is an SPF15. This means a sunscreen which gives you fifteen times more protection that you would have normally. An SPF15 sunscreen will absorb proportionally equal amounts of UVA and UVB, and will give you good protection if you are sensible about your exposure. Sunscreens higher than SPF15 tend to lose their balanced effect: the chemicals in an SPF30, for example, will not block UVA rays as effectively as UVB. The other danger with high SPFs is that people will stay in the sun longer because they think they are better

protected. Higher SPFs do not give proportionately greater protection. An SPF15 gives 93 per cent protection, for example, while an SPF34 gives 97 per cent protection.

F It is vital to apply enough sunscreen. In order to receive the protection offered by an SPF15 sunscreen, you would need to put on a 120 ml bottle every day you spent at the beach. Most people do not use nearly that amount, which will reduce the SPF considerably. Moreover, the effectiveness is likely to diminish further when you perspire or wipe your skin with a towel. You should reapply sun cream at least every hour and after swimming, even if you are using a waterproof brand.

G Only UVA rays can pass through glass, so you won't get sunburnt sitting by a window, while you can still enjoy the warmth of the sun. Be careful when sitting in the shade, however. You can still get burnt because you will be exposed to rays bouncing off reflective surfaces nearby. This is particularly the case near water. Not all clothing offers effective protection, either. If you can see the light through a piece of clothing when you hold it up, it will not offer much of a barrier to UV rays.

H You should keep an eye out for any moles or dark spots on the skin that change in size, shape or colour, become bigger, itchy or inflamed, or bleed. All these may be symptoms of skin cancer and should be checked by a doctor. Once a mole has been identified as a potential melanoma, it is removed under local anaesthetic and sent for examination. Most turn out to be harmless. Of the three forms of skin cancer the two most common varieties – basal cell and squamous cell carcinomas – are easily treatable and rarely fatal, and even melanomas can be treated effectively if caught in time.

Glossary

Cancer – a serious illness caused by a group of cells in the body increasing in an uncontrolled way

Screen out – to prevent something that is dangerous from coming in

Expose – to fail to protect someone or something from something harmful or dangerous

Mole – a dark brown lump or spot on your skin that is permanent

Matching headings to paragraphs

This is a common IELTS task. It will help you understand how the text is organized and can help you identify where to find the information you need to answer the questions about the text.

Reading Passage 1 has eight paragraphs **A–H**. Choose the most suitable heading for paragraphs **B–H** from the list of headings below.

List of headings
i Who is most likely to develop skin cancer?
ii Summer sports and skin protection
iii How the various types of radiation differ ✓
iv Sunscreens: the higher the SPF the better?
v What is ultraviolet radiation? ✓
vi Other ways to protect yourself
vii What are the first signs of skin cancer?
viii Is UV exposure through sunbeds as harmful as natural sunlight? ✓
ix A short break in the sun won't hurt, will it?
x How to maximise the SPF of sunscreens

Pictures, charts and diagrams

1 Complete the table below. Tick if the statement is true for UVA, UVB, or both UVA and UVB radiation.

	UVA	UVB	UVA and UVB
Can lead to skin cancer	✓		•
Causes sunburn		'	
Can lead to premature ageing of the skin			✓
Can pass through glass	•		
Sunbeds use it	•		

2 Label the diagram (below left) with words from the passage.

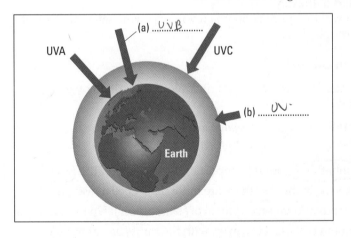

(a) ...U∨B...
UVA
UVC
(b) ...UV...
Earth

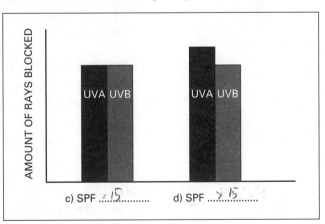

AMOUNT OF RAYS BLOCKED
UVA UVB   UVA UVB
c) SPF =15   d) SPF >15

3 Complete the headings of each bar chart (above right) with the correct numbers.

Multiple choice

1 Exposure to the sun on holiday is dangerous because
   A UVA and UVB rays can lead to skin cancer.
   B we don't usually go out in the sun so much at home.
   C we are exposed to the sun's reflection in the shade.
   D our skins are more exposed in holiday clothes.

2 Sunbeds may be harmful because
   A you won't get sunburnt.
   B you will absorb a large amount of UVA rays.
   C you will get sunburnt.
   D you will be exposed to UVC rays.

3 Moles, or dark spots on the skin
   A are always symptoms of skin cancer.
   B are harmless.
   C should always be checked by a doctor if they change in any way.
   D are becoming more common.

This type of multiple choice question asks you to choose two or three answers from a group of six or seven.

4 Circle **TWO** letters **A–E**.
   Using a high factor (above SPF15) sunscreen can be dangerous because
   A it absorbs equal amounts of UVA and UVB.
   B it will not block UVA as well as it blocks UVB.
   C you will be tempted to stay in the sun longer because you think you are safe.
   D there are more chemicals in it.
   E you will get burnt in the shade.

5 Circle **THREE** letters **A–G**.
   In order for an SPF15 sunscreen to actually offer you 15 times normal protection, you need to
   A be careful of rays reflected from nearby water.
   B make sure you use enough sunscreen.
   C apply the sunscreen again after swimming.
   D cover up with light, loose clothing.
   E avoid the hottest part of the day.
   F remember that you will lose protection when you wipe yourself with a towel.
   G avoid UVA rays through glass.

Guessing meaning from context

1 Look at paragraph A again. Notice how the writer avoids repetition by using synonyms or related words.

sunbathing	→	*lying in the sun*	*melanoma* → *skin cancer*	
risks	→	*dangerous*	*precautions* → *safe*	

A Many people enjoy (sunbathing), but it is important to be aware of the (risks) of (lying in the sun). Every year in the UK, there are more than 4,000 new cases of (melanoma) which is the most (dangerous) form of (skin cancer). Up to 40 per cent of sufferers from melanoma will die. However, with the right (precautions), it is possible to enjoy the sun and still stay (safe).

1 What part of speech is *sufferers*?
2 What will happen to 40 per cent of sufferers? What does this tell you about the word?

2 Look at paragraph F again. Find more words in the paragraph with a similar meaning to those circled.

F It is vital to (apply) enough sunscreen. In order to receive the (protection) offered by an SPF15 sunscreen, you would need to put on a 120 ml bottle every day you spent at the beach. Most people do not <u>use</u> nearly that amount, which will (reduce) the SPF considerably. Moreover, the effectiveness is likely to <u>diminish</u> further when you perspire or wipe your skin with a towel. You should reapply sun cream at least every hour and after swimming, even if you are using a waterproof brand.

Skills practice

Now practise the skills you have learnt by answering the questions on Reading Passage 2.

Reading Passage 2

A While elephants are often one of a zoo's top attractions, a new report charges that their level of care often falls short of star treatment. In a study released this week, the UK's Royal Society for the Protection of Cruelty to Animals (RSPCA) said elephants in European zoos are often unhealthy, endure considerable stress, and have a much shorter life than their counterparts in the wild. Their condition is frequently even worse than that of elephants in Asian timber camps, alleges the RSPCA, which is calling for wide-ranging changes in the way zoo elephants are treated. In the meantime, the group says, European zoos should stop importing and breeding elephants.

B The RSPCA, based in Horsham, England, said it commissioned the study after several high-profile cases of elephant mistreatment, including one in which electric prods were being used to train elephants at a British zoo. The authors collected data on births and deaths from a studbook of elephants at European zoos to assess life expectancy and infant mortality. Studbooks catalogue the family history of animals in captivity, especially to help prevent inbreeding. The studbook spans 40 years of births and deaths for African savanna elephants (*Loxodonta africana*) and nearly 100 years for Asian elephants (*Elephas maximus*) in European zoos. An estimated 500 elephants, 48% of the world's zoo elephant population, are now in zoos across Europe, from Belfast to Paris. Sixty-nine elephants live in UK zoos. The researchers also reviewed more than 100 elephant studies published since 1960, as well as 500 studies on stress biology and the welfare of other captive animals.

C The findings from the demographic data startled the researchers. They found that Asian elephants in European zoos typically live about 15 years, only half as long as elephants in timber camps. Asian elephants can live as long as 65 years in the wild, the researchers said. Rebecca Hawkes, a spokesperson for the RSPCA, said the extensive study "provides compelling, substantiated information that leaves no doubt that elephants' welfare is compromised in European zoos." Elephants have lived in captivity for more than 4,000 years, many of them held in zoos and circuses worldwide. Captive elephants are also used in some Asian countries for timber-logging and in religious ceremonies. Ros Clubb of Oxford University, a zoologist and co-author of the report, said the study was done after "work by other biologists had already set alarm bells ringing." Findings have shown, for example, that 35 per cent of zoo females fail to breed and that 15 to 25 per cent of Asian elephant calves are stillborn. Clubb and her co-author, Georgia Mason, also a zoologist at Oxford University, said females in the wild normally don't conceive until around 18 years of age, but female elephants in zoos often begin breeding as early as age 12, putting them and their offspring at higher risk of death and illness. The researchers also found that zoo elephants are often overweight—up to 50 per cent heavier than their counterparts in the wild—and commonly exhibit unusual behaviour such as weaving to and fro.

D Mason said such conditions likely stem from a combination of ill health, unusually small social groupings, inadequate dwelling space, and European weather that is often colder than in the elephants' native habitats. Female elephants in the wild live in interactive family groups of up to ten individuals, said Mason. The female calves usually remain in their family group for life and develop strong bonds with members of that group. In contrast, zoo elephants are typically found in groups of two, and two-thirds of female calves are taken from their mothers at an early age. This low level of family structure and the relatively small enclosures of zoos contribute to boredom and distress, said Mason. Wild elephants roam over distances as much as 60 to 100 times larger than typical housing for zoo elephants, 90% of whom have no natural grazing.

E Although the RSPCA-sponsored study was limited to European zoos, Mason believes the findings may be widely applicable. "Studies of US zoos certainly show that they too have had problems with high [elephant] infant mortality," she said, adding that researchers should "look to see if similar things are happening there."

F Lori Eggert, who studies elephant genetics and behaviour at the Smithsonian Institution in Washington, DC, agreed that it's important to ensure zoo elephants' comfort and welfare but said meeting the demands called for in the study would be challenging. "Elephants [in the wild] require lots of room, and trying to closely mimic their natural habitat or large social groups would be very difficult," she said.

G The Federation of Zoological Gardens of Great Britain and Ireland said in a statement that its members remained committed to improving the welfare of their elephants. "Given the bleak outlook for elephants in the wild, zoo elephants have an increasingly valuable role to play," the statement said. Apart from their drawing power as major wildlife attractions, zoo elephants are important for conservation, research, and public education. "Elephants are generally used as a flagship species," said Eggert. "As such, they inspire awe and love for nature in people and further inspire them to open their pocketbooks to give money for conservation of habitats."

H Eggert said working with zoo elephants was indispensable to her own research achievements. Much understanding about animal biology and behaviour, such as forms of communication and patterns of reproduction, have been based on research involving elephants and other zoo animals, providing research opportunities that would be difficult or impossible in the world, Eggert explained. "There are a lot of strong beliefs out there, but now we need real, objective data on what captive elephants need," said Mason. "Only then," she added, "can we judge whether zoos can ever reliably keep these animals well."

Glossary
Mistreat – to treat someone in an unfair or cruel way
In captivity – in a zoo or park
Inadequate dwelling space – not enough room to live
Breeding – producing young animals
Timber logging – cutting down trees for wood
Grazing – grass areas which animals can eat from

Question 1

Choose the most appropriate heading for Reading Passage 2 from the list below.

List of headings
  i Elephants born in captivity are mistreated
  ii Zoo life in Europe shortens elephant lives
  iii Wild elephants more intelligent than those in zoos

Questions 2–4

Reading Passage 2 has eight paragraphs **A–H**. Choose the most appropriate headings for paragraphs **B**, **C** and **D** from the list below.

List of headings
  i Arguments in favour of keeping elephants in zoos
  ii Inadequate living space for elephants in zoos
  iii The importance of research into elephants
  iv Specific problems of zoo elephants in Europe
  v Possible reasons for the study's findings
  vi Worldwide implications of the study
  vii How and why the study was carried out

2   Paragraph B   3   Paragraph C   4   Paragraph D ....

Questions 5–8

Complete the table below. Choose **NO MORE THAN THREE WORDS OR A NUMBER** from Reading Passage 2 for each answer.

	Life span	Age start breeding	Typical size of family group
Elephants in zoos	15	(5) *as young as*	2
Elephants in the wild	(6) *as old as*	18	(7) *as many as* ....
Elephants in timber camps	(8) *usually only around*		

Questions 9–11

Which **THREE** reasons are given for why it is important to keep elephants in zoos?

List of reasons
A providing opportunities to understand more about animals through research
B attracting the public to zoos
C protecting elephants from having to work in timber logging
D helping to get people interested in animals and nature
E to keep elephant families together
F teaching elephants to do amusing tricks
G to give the elephants plenty of room

9   Reason 1 ....   10 Reason 2 ....   11 Reason 3 ....

Questions 12–14

Label the charts. Choose your answers from the box below.

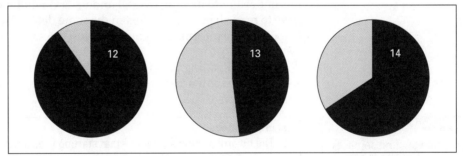

Proportion of:
A European zoo elephants without grazing
B European zoo elephants held in UK zoos
C European female zoo elephants separated very early from their mothers
D World zoo elephants held in Europe
E European female zoo elephants who fail to breed

Questions 15–17

Circle the appropriate letters **A–C**.

15 According to Lori Eggert, imitating elephants' natural habitat in a zoo would be difficult because
   A the weather is colder in Europe.
   B the elephants would need too much space.
   C the elephants are needed for research.

16 According to Georgia Mason, not being with members of their family makes the elephants feel
   A bored and unhappy.
   B aggressive.
   C hungry.

17 According to Ros Clubb, the study was undertaken
   A because no one had investigated the area before.
   B to find out why zoo elephants are often overweight.
   C after previous research had shown possible problems for zoo elephants.

Reading Passages 3 and 4

Skills development

Skimming for gist

The heading of Reading Passage 3 is *A Burning Question*. This means that people have strong opinions about a question and think it is very important. Skim the text and decide what the burning question is. Choose the best explanation from **A–C**.

A Who is to blame for causing bushfires?
B What is the best way to prevent bushfires burning out of control?
C Why does Australia have more bushfires than Canada?

Scanning to find information quickly

It is important to have an overall understanding of the text but you do not always have to read all parts of the text in the same detail. If you can quickly identify where to look for the information you need, you can save a lot of time.

1 Read the Reading Passage 3 in no more than four minutes. Match each paragraph **A–E** with the sentences **i–v** below which summarize their content. Check your answers on page 76.

Remember
Try reading the first sentence of each paragraph. This is usually the topic sentence, or the sentence that introduces the main topic of the paragraph. If this does not help you, try looking at the last sentence instead, particularly when looking at the first and last paragraphs of a newspaper or magazine article.

List of sentences
 i The environmentalists' view – that starting fires deliberately destroys the environment.
 ii The scientists' point of view – that bushfires are natural and necessary and should be deliberately started each year in a controlled way.
 iii Why environmentalists think the fires are getting worse (global warming) – and why scientists think they aren't (they just seem worse because more people live near the bush now).
 iv Introducing the topic and telling the reader that there is an argument about the causes of bushfires and how to stop them.
 v What people should do to prevent the fires spreading when they build their houses and gardens near the bush.

A burning question

A   The bushfires came to Melbourne today in a more gentle manner than usual. No firestorms raging close to suburban streets and houses reduced to ash – just a sooty cloud that drifted down from the mountains and hung over the city for the day. For Australians, this counts as a quiet period for bushfires. Tens of thousands of hectares of national park may be disappearing in smoke, but few people are under direct threat. The national park recovers; homes don't. But in the lull between backyard infernos, battle has been rejoined on the contentious issue of what is causing the bushfires, and how they can be stopped.

B   Environmentalists are pitted against a growing body of scientists who say the only way to limit the blazes is to set the bush on fire during the winter months. "There's this misunderstanding of the nature of fire," said Phil Cheney, of the Commonwealth Scientific and Industrial Research Organisation (CSIRO). "Most people still don't accept that it's a natural ecological phenomenon, and until we do that we're not going to be able to prevent these out-of-control fires." Australian species such as the eucalyptus and banksia often require the passage of bushfires to allow their seeds to germinate, and the characteristic bark-shedding of eucalyptus is believed to have evolved to provide tinder on the forest floor.

C   But John Connor, Campaigns Director of the Australian Conservation Foundation, disagrees that burnoffs on national park land are the answer. "Of course you need some sort of burning close to houses, but then every summer we hear these people who just want to concrete over the place," he says. Bushfires may be natural, he says, but the sort of forest management needed to prevent risk to property is definitely not. "A lot of native plants can survive maybe three fires in 20 years, but more often than that and you'll end up with nothing but eucalyptus in the forest," he said.

D   Environmentalists believe the real concern around the fires should be the indication they give of the coming impact of global warming – a view backed up by greenhouse experts such as Ian Noble, formerly of the Australian National University. But so far there is little reliable information to indicate whether fires have in fact been getting worse, and many scientists, such as Jim Gould of the CSIRO's bushfire behaviour and management centre, say that there hasn't even been an increase. "More and more people are living in the bushland, and they expect the same level of protection as if they lived in the city," he said. "So you hear a lot more about the fires because there's more people living cheek-by-jowl with the fire areas." The urban areas of Sydney and Melbourne have doubled since 1960, and – particularly in Sydney – much of the development has been in long arms stretching deep into the bush country. The three areas worst affected by the fires that hit Sydney before Christmas were all on the bush fringes and had seen a massive influx of city-dwellers in recent years, keen to escape the inner city and enjoy the pleasures of the bush.

E   Phil Cheney says there has been no measurable change in the incidence of fires since the 1960s, when he remembers flying 600 km (373 miles) between Bega, near the Victorian border, and Newcastle, north of Sydney, and seeing only two breaks in the continuous fire front. "The provision of an implicit guarantee of protection from the emergency services has meant that people are moving into these dangerous areas and are not taking any of the precautions which they should be taking," he says. Many dwellers on the bush fringe choose to make the most of their new location by planting gardens using flammable native plants, rather than the more retardant imported species, and building homes on the tops of ridges to enjoy the views of bushland. These last are a particular fire risk, as winds can fan fireballs up the steep wooded slopes and consume the houses on top with breathtaking speed. Meeka Bailey of the New South Wales Rural Fire Service says that new planning rules passed in New South Wales in August should make some difference, but will do little to improve the situation in areas which have already been built up. "People need to put space between their houses and the forest, keep away from the higher areas and clear out dry undergrowth from their gardens, otherwise it will only encourage the fires," she said.

Glossary

Bush – areas in hot countries that are not used for growing food

Blaze – a large fire that causes a lot of damage

Flammable – likely to burn very quickly and easily

Environmentalist – someone who wants to protect the environment

Climate change/global warming – the changes that are thought to be affecting the world's weather, making it warmer

Greenhouse effect – the process in which heat is unable to escape from the atmosphere and causes the temperature of the Earth to rise

Ridge – the long narrow top of a mountain

Fringe – the outer edge of something

2 Read questions **1–3**. Before you answer them, decide in which paragraph **A–E** you will find the answer. Don't look back at the text at this stage, though you can look back at the summarizing sentences in exercise 1 if necessary.

1 How does the scientist, Phil Cheney, describe the nature of fire?
2 What kind of people have recently moved to the bush fringe around Sydney?
3 In what position is it particularly dangerous to build your home on the bush fringe?

3 Scan the text again to check you have chosen the correct paragraph.

Short answer questions

Look at extracts **i–iii** from Reading Passage 3 and answer questions **1–3**. <u>Underline</u> any words that will answer each question.

1 How does the scientist, Phil Cheney, describe the nature of fire?
2 What kind of people have recently moved to the bush fringe around Sydney?
3 In what position is it particularly dangerous to build your home on the bush fringe?

i "There's this misunderstanding of the nature of fire," said Phil Cheney, of the Commonwealth Scientific and Industrial Research Organisation (CSIRO). "Most people still don't accept that it's a natural ecological phenomenon, and until we do that we're not going to be able to prevent these out-of-control fires."

ii The three areas worst affected by the fires that hit Sydney before Christmas were all on the bush fringes and had seen a massive influx of city-dwellers in recent years, keen to escape the inner city and enjoy the pleasures of the bush.

iii Many dwellers on the bush fringe choose to make the most of their new location by planting gardens using flammable native plants, rather than the more retardant imported species, and building homes on the tops of ridges to enjoy the views of bushland. These last are a particular fire risk, as winds can fan fireballs up the steep wooded slopes and consume the houses on top with breathtaking speed.

Remember
- Check the question specifies that you should use words from the passage.

Remember
- You do not necessarily need to include articles in your three words, eg *(a) natural ecological phenomenon.*
- Sometimes you can only understand a sentence properly when you read the next one or the one before. Look at extract i: *it's* refers to *fire*. Look at extract iii: it is only clear that building houses on the tops of ridges is dangerous if you read on and understand that *these last* refers back to homes *on the tops of ridges*. Look out for referring expressions like *the former, the latter, this,* etc. as well as pronouns such as *they, his,* etc. and make sure you know what they refer to.

Understanding paraphrasing

Look at the way the extracts from the text below have been rewritten using different words (paraphrased). Is the meaning the same or different?
If the meaning is different, change the paraphrase to make the meaning the same as the extract.

Extract	Paraphrase
1 The bushfires came to Melbourne today in a more gentle manner than usual. No firestorms raging close to suburban streets and houses reduced to ash …	Houses were destroyed by bushfires in Melbourne on the day the article was written.
2 More and more people are living in the bushland … a massive influx of city-dwellers.	There has been a large increase in the number of people from the cities moving into the bush.
3 'Of course you need some sort of burning close to houses …' (says John Connor)	John Connor agrees that limited burning just near people's property is necessary.
4 Environmentalists are pitted against a growing body of scientists who say the only way to limit the blazes is to set the bush on fire during the winter months.	All scientists disagree with environmentalists about the best way to limit the blazes.

True, False or *Not Given* and *Yes, No* or *Not Given*

Do the following statements agree with the information given in Reading Passage 3?
Write:

YES	if the statement agrees with the information given
NO	if the statement contradicts the information given
NOT GIVEN	if there is no information about this

1 Some Australian species of animals need bushfires to survive.
2 People like to build their houses on the top of ridges.
3 Many Australian plants can survive three fires a year.
4 Bushfires have in fact been getting worse.
5 What the fires may suggest about future climate change is the most worrying thing for environmentalists.
6 People are dying in bushfires every year.

If your answer was *Yes* or *No*, <u>underline</u> the words in the passage which gave you the information.

Recognizing opinion

The reading passages in the IELTS exam often contain both fact and opinion.

1 Read statements **1–5** below. According to Reading Passage 3, which are facts and which are opinions? Write **F** for fact or **O** for opinion next to each statement.

1 Hundreds of miles of land can be on fire during an Australian bushfire. …………
2 Burning parkland deliberately is the answer to controlling these fires. …………
3 There are twice as many people living in the Sydney and Melbourne areas now than there were in the 1960s. …………
4 There has been no real change in the number of bushfires since the 1960s. …………
5 The real concern about these fires is how they show us what the effects of global warming will be. …………

Remember
- You are unlikely to find exactly the same phrases or words used in the passage. Find something which says the same thing in different words.
- Something may be obviously true or false, but not mentioned in the passage. Always check that you can find evidence in the passage for your answer and if you can't, choose the *Not Given* option.

2 Classify opinions **1–5** below as belonging to

John Connor	**JC**
Phil Cheney	**PC**
Jim Gould	**JG**
Meeka Bailey	**MB**

1 There is more in the news about bushfires because more people live near the bush now.
2 Building houses too close to the bush is dangerous.
3 Although bushfires happen naturally, setting them deliberately is not a good idea.
4 The only way to prevent fires getting out of control is to accept that fires are a natural part of bush life.
5 People don't realise the danger they are in from bushfires.

3 In Reading Passage 3, the writer's main purpose is

1 to give advice on avoiding the spread of bushfires.
2 to persuade environmentalists of the necessity for regular controlled fires.
3 to present different arguments on the subject of how best to control bushfires.
4 to give a history of the spread of bushfires in Australia.

Skills practice

Now practise the skills you have learnt by answering the questions on Reading Passage 4.

Reading Passage 4

Do you know how much salt you're eating?

A What did you feed your child yesterday? Cornflakes for breakfast, perhaps? Marmite sandwiches for lunch? For supper, beans on toast, with a packet of crisps as a snack somewhere in between? The menu will vary from household to household, but the chances are that you will have fed your child, and yourself, at least twice as much salt as the recommended maximum level. Despite growing awareness of the health risks involved with high salt intake, the Food Commission reports this week that many products, especially those aimed at children, are saltier than they were 25 years ago.

B So what are the long-term consequences for our health – and why is there so much salt in our diet? Salt has long been considered a magical substance. In Ancient Rome, it was considered so important to health that a soldier's pay included a special allowance which had to be spent on salt. In the chilly climes of northern Europe, before the development of refrigeration, salt provided one of the few ways of preserving foods to get families through the winter. And it is well known that a small amount – a tiny amount – is vital for our bodies to function properly, to keep nerve pathways working and maintain our muscles. But in a culture hooked on convenience, processed food, 90% of the population is heavily overdosing on salt which they probably don't even realise is in there.

C The Food Commission, which is the UK's leading independent watchdog on food issues, studied the ingredients in white bread, crisps, baked beans and canned tomato soup, comparing the salt content in 1978 with equivalent products selling today. Among the most shocking of their findings was the discovery that salt in crisps has almost doubled since 1978, from an average of 540 mg per 100 g to 1050 mg per 100 g. In the rest, there was little improvement, despite industry and government claims that salt has been cut in these processed foods.

D Graham MacGregor, who is professor of cardiovascular medicine at St George's Hospital, in south London, is an expert on salt. In the past, concern about salt intake has focused mainly on the middle-aged with high blood pressure and heart trouble, but according to MacGregor all of us are eating much too much salt, and the consequences for our health could be dramatic. "On average we are eating 10–12 grammes of salt a day," he says. "The recommended maximum intake for an adult is 5–6 grammes (one flat teaspoonful). Ninety per cent of the population exceed that, which puts up blood pressure in everybody, which is the major cause of strokes and heart attacks in this country. It's a very major problem. "If we did reduce total salt intake by the recommended amounts, it would save approximately 30,000 heart attacks and strokes in the UK every year."

E In addition to high blood pressure, strokes and heart attacks, which are two of the most common causes of death and illness in the UK, high salt intake is also associated with osteoporosis, fluid retention, asthma and stomach cancer. The risk is particularly acute in children, who are subjected to intensive marketing of snack and fast-food products that are exorbitantly high in salt. The government's Scientific Advisory Committee on Nutrition (SACN) has recommended that children under seven years should consume an average of not more than two grammes of salt a day. Those between seven and 14 should consume not more than five grammes. "The furring of the arteries starts in early childhood, and children are now eating this appalling diet which is very high in salt," says MacGregor. "People are much less aware they are eating it, but it's all hidden in these processed foods. We are talking about foods that are 20–30% more salty than sea water." As much as 80% of the salt in our diet comes from processed foods, but why do salt levels need to be so high? "Because it's completely inedible without it. It's totally tasteless," says MacGregor. "It's to cover up," agrees Anton Edelmann, head chef at the Savoy hotel in London. "It makes up for poor ingredients. It also works as a stabiliser in some foods; it retains the moisture in the food, and keeps it a little bit longer."

F Other conspiracy theorists speculate about the links between producers of snack foods and soft drinks – crisp manufacturer Walkers, for example, is a division of PepsiCo which produces Pepsi Cola. Salty foods lead to thirsty children, which in turn leads to increased sales of soft drinks, they suggest. Steve Chandler of the Snack, Nut and Crisp Manufacturers' Association, which represents companies such as Walkers, KP (makers of Hula Hoops) and Golden Wonder, yesterday dismissed such theories as "total nonsense" and claimed that in the past 10 years, the industry had worked hard to reduce salt levels, which escalated in the late 1970s and 80s with a massive increase in the number and variety of snack products on the market. "We've managed to pull it back to the tune of 25% over the past 10 years," he says. "We do listen to what the expert advice is. We do listen to what consumers say. We put a lot of time and effort into trying to improve the nutritional aspects of our product."

G The good news is that public awareness is growing. Anton Edelmann used to see customers furiously shaking salt over food he had meticulously flavoured and seasoned in his kitchen. "That's gone nowadays. People are more aware of the fact they should not eat too much salt, but they don't know how to reduce it. In an ideal world I would remove the salt cellar from the table, but I can't do that. We all eat more processed food, and that's where the problem comes in. You can't control how much salt you're eating. How can you fight this avalanche of processed foods? People say they have less time so they cook less and buy more ready-meals. I think they should work an hour less and go home and cook proper food."

H Tomorrow is National Salt Awareness Day. What a great day to take Anton's advice, knock off early and get home to the cooker.

Glossary

Convenience foods – food that is quick and easy to prepare

Processed foods – food which has chemicals added to keep it fresh

Heart attack – an occasion when someone suddenly has a lot of pain in their chest and their heart stops working

Stroke – a medical condition when blood is suddenly blocked and cannot reach the brain, so you can't move some muscles, or speak

Osteoporosis – a medical condition when your bones become more likely to break

Fluid retention – a medical condition when parts of your body swell because of extra fluid, or liquid

Asthma – a medical condition that makes it difficult to breathe

High blood pressure – a medical condition when the pressure of blood flowing from your heart is too high

Questions 1–4

Reading Passage 4 has seven paragraphs **A–H**. Which paragraphs include the following information? Write the appropriate letters.

1   What the producers of snack food say about the amount of salt in their products. ....
2   Why salt is important in our diet. ....
3   The writer's opinion and reason for writing the article. ....
4   Medical problems associated with salt. ....

Questions 5–8

Write **NO MORE THAN THREE WORDS OR A NUMBER** for each answer.

5   What type of food typically provides 80% of the salt in our diet?

    ....

6   What percentage of the UK population is eating too much salt?

    ....

7   What is the maximum amount of salt that children under seven

    should eat each day? ....

8   Which two health problems does MacGregor say can be a result of high blood

    pressure? .... and ....

Questions 9–12

Do the following statements agree with the information given in Reading Passage 4? Write:

TRUE   if the statement is true according to the passage
FALSE   if the statement is false according to the passage
NOT GIVEN   if there is no information about this

 9 People are increasingly aware of the need to reduce the amount of salt they eat.
10 High salt intake only affects your heart and blood pressure.
11 In Ancient Roman times soldiers spent a lot of money on salt.
12 Our bodies need a little salt to work properly.

Questions 13–17

Classify statements **13–17** as:

a finding of the Food Commission study   **FC**
a claim of the crisp and snack manufacturers   **CSM**
a scientist's opinion   **SO**
a chef's opinion   **CO**

13 Salt in crisps and snacks has been reduced by 25% over the last 10 years.
14 It is more important to eat healthily than to save time.
15 People from all age groups are eating too much salt.
16 There is almost twice as much salt in crisps now than in 1978.
17 Crisp manufacturers do not produce salty food to encourage children to buy more soft drinks.

Question 18

Circle the appropriate letter.

The writer of the article thinks we should

A feed our children more salt than the recommended maximum level.
B cook our own food rather than eat processed food.
C eat no more than 5–6 grammes a day of salt.
D increase the number of snacks on the market.

Skills development

Skimming for gist

Quickly read Reading Passage 5. Choose the best summary **A–D** of the findings of Brodsky's research.

A Driving too fast causes more deaths on the road.
B Listening to loud music while driving causes more accidents.
C Music in cars is distracting to drivers, especially when it's fast and loud.
D People listen to music in the car more often than anywhere else.

Reading Passage 5

Speed kills. But it is not only the speed at which people drive that is the problem: the speed of the music they are listening to also has a hand in their fate. An Israeli researcher says drivers who listen
5 to fast music in their cars may have more than twice as many accidents as those listening to slower tracks.

With the car now the place where people most often listen to music, the research is worrying.
10 While previous studies have shown a link between loud music and dangerous driving, Warren Brodsky at Ben-Gurion University in Beer-Sheva, wondered if tempo had any effect on driver behaviour. To find out, he put a group of 28
15 students through their paces on a driving simulator.

Each student drove round the virtual streets of Chicago while listening to different pieces of music, or none at all. The students had an average
20 of seven years' driving experience.

Brodsky chose music with a variety of styles, ranging from laid-back George Benson ballads to the ultra-fast numbers beloved of clubbers. The tempo ranged from a slow 60 beats per minute up
25 to a fast and furious 120 beats per minute or more. All the music was played relatively loudly to maximise its effect.

As the tempo increased, Brodsky found drivers ran more risks, such as jumping red lights, and
30 had more accidents. When listening to up-tempo pieces, they were twice as likely to jump a red light as those who were not listening to music. And

drivers had more than twice as many accidents when they were listening to fast tempos as when
35 they listened to slow or medium-paced numbers. Brodsky concedes that behaviour on a simulator may not translate into the same behaviour on the road. "But I think it's got to be taken seriously," he says.

40 He also monitored the drivers' heart rate and found that it fluctuated less when they were listening to music of any kind compared with no music at all. This lack of variation, he suggests, shows that music is distracting the drivers and
45 making them less alert.

So what should drivers do? Brodsky says they should be aware of the tempo effect and choose slower pieces of music – or turn down the volume so they are less distracted.

50 The study has changed Brodsky's own attitude to in-car music. He chose the pieces that he used in the study after listening to them as he drove to work. "I could hardly control myself with some of the pieces. It was difficult taking my foot off the
55 gas pedal," he says. "I'm now more careful in my choice of music."

"Very little research has been carried out into how people's lifestyles affect their driving behaviour," says Roger Vincent of Britain's Royal Society for
60 the Prevention of Accidents. "We need more research into the effects of distractions in cars."

Glossary
Alert – paying attention to what is happening and being ready to react if necessary
Lack of – to not have any or enough of something you need or want
Distracting – preventing you from concentrating

Summary completion

1 Read at the summary and decide what part of speech each gap is (noun, verb, adjective, etc.).

Brodsky investigated the effect of the (1) .... of music on driver behaviour.

(2) .... used a driving simulator while listening to different kinds of music.

Brodsky found that fast music caused drivers to take more (3) .... but any music was more (4) .... than none.

risks   students   time
speed   type   motivating
care   fluctuating
distracting   alert
researchers

2 Complete the summary with words from the box. Note that there are more words than spaces, so you do not need to use them all.

Guessing meaning from context

In the previous exercise we saw how a word from the text (*tempo*) was replaced with a synonym (*speed*). There may also be some clues in the sentences around the new word. Look at these sentences:

Brodsky chose music with a variety of styles, **ranging from laid-back George Benson ballads to the ultra-fast numbers** beloved of clubbers. The **tempo ranged from a slow 60 beats per minute up to a fast and furious 120 beats per minute** or more.

These two sentences together make it clear that the writer is describing speed and help you to guess the meaning of the word *tempo*.

1 Look at Reading Passage 5 again and find words which mean the same as definitions **1–6** below.

1 not real but created by a computer
2 calm and relaxed
3 admit that something is true
4 to check regularly or measure something to find out what is happening
5 changed frequently
6 someone's opinions about something, especially as shown by their behaviour

2 Underline the other words in the text which helped you guess correctly.

Note completion

Notes often list key points about the passage or part of a passage.

Complete the notes below. Choose **ONE OR TWO WORDS** from Reading Passage 5 for each answer.

According to Brodsky, drivers are not so (1) .... because music affects their concentration.
So, drivers should: play music which is (2) ....
               ensure they do not become (3) .... by turning down the volume.

Understanding paraphrasing and sentence completion

1 Look back at the first four paragraphs of Reading Passage 5 and find phrases or sentences with the same meaning as **1–5** below.

1 is involved in what happens to them
2 the results of the study should concern us
3 got them to show how good they were
4 at quite a high volume
5 to make something as effective as possible

2 Choose **ONE** phrase from **A–I** below to complete sentences **1–3**.

1 The speed at which people drive …
2 The fastest music played in the study was …
3 Listening to fast music while driving …

List of phrases	
A laid-back George Benson ballads	**F** is not the only problem
B jumped a red light	**G** more than 120 beats per minute
C to maximise their effect	**H** is not a problem
D is the problem	**I** doubled the number of accidents
E 60 beats a minute	

3 Complete the sentences below with words from Reading Passage 5. Write **NO MORE THAN THREE WORDS OR A NUMBER** for each answer.

1 Safer drivers listened to ....

2 On average the students had been driving ....

3 To increase its impact the music was ....

4 Slow or .... tracks were safer than faster pieces of music.

Skills practice

Now practise the skills you have learnt by answering the questions on Reading Passage 6.

Reading Passage 6

An oil frequently found on your bathroom shelf may prove a viable alternative to diesel fuel for cars and trucks. Early tests show that jojoba-fuelled engines kick out fewer
5 pollutants, run more quietly and for longer, and perform just as well as diesels.

The search for alternative fuels, driven by dwindling oil reserves and concerns over exhaust emissions, has led researchers to
10 investigate more sustainable sources such as vegetable oils. Sunflower oil, soybean oil and even opium poppy oil have all been tested as potential fuels.

Now it is jojoba's turn. Jojoba is a desert
15 shrub that can reach up to 4.5 metres high and typically lives more than 150 years, producing nuts that yield half their volume in oil. The non-toxic oil is widely used as a non-greasy skin-smoothing ingredient in
20 cosmetics, and as a base for shampoos and make-up.

Engineers think the oil has potential as a motor fuel because it releases a lot of energy when it burns and is chemically stable at the
25 high temperatures and pressures in a working engine.

To test jojoba in engines, Mohamed Selim and his colleagues at the United Arab Emirates University in Al-Ain and at the
30 Helwan University in Cairo, connected an array of sensors to a diesel engine and monitored its performance while burning regular diesel fuel. They then ran the engine on a fuel called jojoba methyl ester, which
35 they made simply by adding a dash of methanol and a catalyst to raw jojoba oil.

Selim's team reveals in the journal *Renewable Energy* (vol 28, p. 1401) that the jojoba fuel matched diesel for torque and power over
40 the engine speeds they tested, between 1000 and 2000 revolutions per minute. What is more, the jojoba combustion gases took slightly longer to reach maximum pressure in the cylinder, which Selim believes may
45 explain why the engine runs more quietly on the nut oil.

Selim says jojoba is worth pursuing as an alternative fuel because it contains less carbon than fuels like diesel, which means
50 lower emissions of carbon monoxide, carbon dioxide and soot. And unlike diesel, jojoba oil contains no sulphur, so not only will the exhaust be free of harmful sulphur oxides, but the cylinders will be spared exposure to
55 corrosive sulphuric acid, so the engine will last longer. Jojoba also has a higher 'flashpoint' than diesel, meaning it is less likely to explode while being stored or transported.

60 Of course, growing enough jojoba would be a huge challenge. "The use of jojoba as a fuel needs huge quantities of seeds, which needs large investment, probably by the government or private sector," says Selim.
65 But while jojoba is unlikely to challenge diesel globally, it could gain popularity in certain regions. It can be grown in hot climates, salty soils and even deserts. "It needs to be cultivated in huge amounts,
70 which is easy in the desert lands in many countries," he says. The plant has been grown for decades in the American south-west and north-west Mexico. It is now cultivated throughout South America and in
75 several Middle East countries. Arable farmers in Egypt have already started planting jojoba shrubs specifically to use the nut oil as a fuel.

Questions 1–4

Complete the summary below with words from the box. You will not need to use all the words.

a sustainable source   diesel   an alternative   petrol   safer   the nut oil
cultivate   a fuel   manufacture   globally   cheaper

Jojoba has been found to have potential as (1) .... to diesel

fuel. Scientists found that jojoba was as powerful as (2) ....

and that it was also cleaner and (3) .... It will be easiest to

(4) .... in desert lands.

Questions 5–8

Complete the summary below. Choose **ONE** word from the last paragraph of Reading Passage 6 for each answer.

Jojoba is easy to grow, even in (5) .... However, very large

(6) .... are needed to use it as fuel, requiring a significant (7) ....

Nonetheless, farmers in Egypt are already growing jojoba plants (8) ....

for this purpose.

Questions 9–11

Choose one phrase from **A–H** below to complete sentences **9–11**.

 9 Engines using fuel made from jojoba ....
10 Diesel oil ....
11 The desert shrub jojoba ....

List of phrases
A contains more carbon monoxide than alternative fuels
B contains no sulphur
C needs plenty of water
D is now cultivated throughout South America
E have been tested as potential fuels all over the world
F are less polluting than diesel
G release a lot of energy
H is unlikely to challenge diesel globally

Questions 12–14

Choose one word or phrase **A–G** to complete sentences **12–14**.

12 Dwindling oil reserves have led people to look for ....

13 The scientists found that the diesel and the jojoba were equally ....

14 Jojoba is safer to transport than diesel because it is not as likely to ....

List of words/phrases
A powerful
B jojoba oil
C alternative fuels
D damage
E explode
F clean
G popular

Questions 15 and 16

Complete each of the statements below with words from Reading Passage 6. Write **NO MORE THAN THREE WORDS** for each answer.

15 Apart from jojoba, an example of an alternative fuel source that has been

   investigated is ....

16 Dangerous emissions from diesel exhaust fumes include

   ....

Study Skills: Writing

How much do you know about the IELTS Academic Writing module?

Do the quiz below to find out.

Quiz

1. How long is the Writing module?
   - **A** 90 minutes   **B** 60 minutes
   - **C** 50 minutes

2. Complete the table.

	How long should you spend on this task?	Minimum number of words
Task 1		
Task 2		

3. In Task 1 what do you have to do?
   - **A** present your opinions
   - **B** describe facts and data
   - **C** write a story

4. In Task 1 what do you have to write?
   - **A** a report for a university lecturer
   - **B** an informal letter to a friend
   - **C** a description of an event

5. In Task 2 what do you have to do?
   - **A** present and justify your opinions
   - **B** describe a historical event
   - **C** compare and contrast photographs

6. In Task 2 what do you have to write?
   - **A** a report
   - **B** a formal letter to a company
   - **C** an essay or composition

Writing Task 1

In Task 1 you will be asked to describe visual data, for example a chart, graph or table in at least 150 words.

Skills development

Understanding data

1 Look at the figures **1–4** and identify which one is:

1. a line graph
2. a bar chart
3. a table
4. a pie chart

2 Look at labels **A–F** and identify:

1. vertical axes
2. horizontal axes
3. columns
4. a row
5. a segment showing a quarter
6. a segment showing just over a third

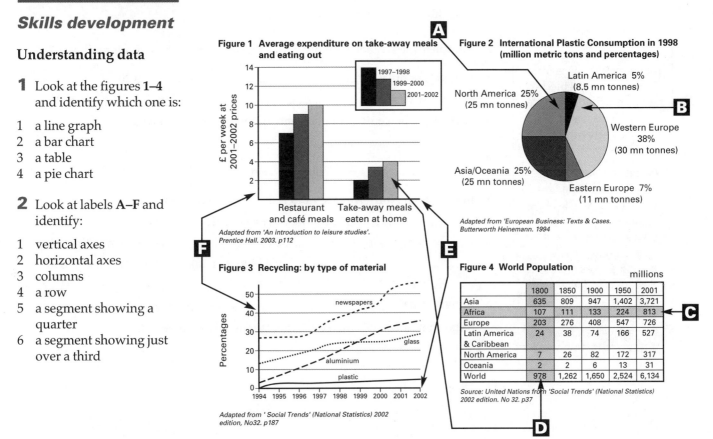

Figure 1 Average expenditure on take-away meals and eating out

Adapted from 'An introduction to leisure studies'. Prentice Hall. 2003. p112

Figure 2 International Plastic Consumption in 1998 (million metric tons and percentages)

North America 25% (25 mn tonnes)
Latin America 5% (8.5 mn tonnes)
Western Europe 38% (30 mn tonnes)
Eastern Europe 7% (11 mn tonnes)
Asia/Oceania 25% (25 mn tonnes)

Adapted from 'European Business: Texts & Cases. Butterworth Heinemann. 1994

Figure 3 Recycling: by type of material

Adapted from ' Social Trends' (National Statistics) 2002 edition, No32. p187

Figure 4 World Population

	1800	1850	1900	1950	2001
Asia	635	809	947	1,402	3,721
Africa	107	111	133	224	813
Europe	203	276	408	547	726
Latin America & Caribbean	24	38	74	166	527
North America	7	26	82	172	317
Oceania	2	2	6	13	31
World	978	1,262	1,650	2,524	6,134

millions

Source: United Nations from 'Social Trends' (National Statistics) 2002 edition. No 32. p37

3 Which figure **1–4** tells you about:

1 the amount of plastic used?
2 the number of people living in different continents?
3 the percentage of waste materials recycled?
4 eating habits?

4 Look at figures **1–4** again and find the answers to these questions.

Figure 1 1 What type of eating was most popular in 2001?
          2 What do the figures on the vertical axis represent?
Figure 2 1 Which area consumed the most plastic in 1998?
          2 How much plastic did Eastern Europe consume?
Figure 3 1 What period of time is shown on this graph?
          2 Which materials were recycled most in 2002?
Figure 4 1 What does the column on the left refer to?
          2 What does the row at the bottom refer to?

Language focus: Expressing figures and quantities

1 Now complete these sentences. Refer to figures **1–4**.

1 On average, between 1997 and 1998 about .... per week was spent on eating at restaurants and cafés compared to about .... on takeaways.

2 Latin America consumed the least amount of plastic in .... at .... million tonnes.

3 Aluminium recycling increased steadily from about .... in 1994 to well over .... in 2002.

4 In 1800 approximately .... million people lived in North America but in 2001 this figure had risen to .... million.

2 Complete the sentences below with a phrase from the box. Refer to figures **1–4**.

exactly the same
much more   very little
more than trebled
half as much   a quarter
twice as many
slightly more

1 Europe's population .... from 1800 to 2001.

2 Oceania had over .... people in 1950 as it did in 1900.

3 In 1999, the percentage of glass and aluminium recycled was ....

4 .... plastic was recycled in 1994.

5 In 1998, both North America and Asia/Oceania consumed .... of the world's plastic.

6 Eastern Europe consumed .... plastic than Latin America.

7 .... money was spent on takeaway meals in 1997–1998 as it was in 2001–2002.

8 In 2001–2002, ... money was spent on eating in restaurants and cafés than on eating takeaways at home.

Remember
- Take time to read and understand the title of the diagram.
- Check you understand what the vertical and horizontal axes represent.
- Be careful to describe the data correctly.
- Compare and contrast figures in different ways.

The opening statement

Here is a simple outline of a Task 1 answer:
- opening statement
- general information and most significant trends
- more specific information and evidence of significant trends

It is important that the first sentence of your answer shows that you understand the information shown in the diagram(s).

1 Look at the bar chart. Which of the sentences **A–D** below is the most appropriate opening sentence? Why?

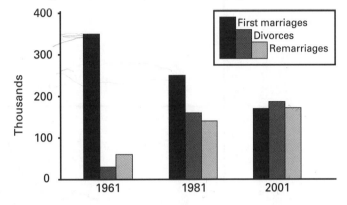

Marriages and Divorces in the United Kingdom

Adapted from 'Social Trends' (National Statistics) 2002 edition. No 32. p43

A This bar chart shows the number of marriages and divorces in the UK.
B This bar chart proves that weddings are not as popular as they used to be and people often get married when they are older.
C The chart shows that the number of first marriages decreased in the period 1961–2001, while figures for divorces and remarriages increased.
D The chart clearly illustrates that the number of first marriages has risen and the number of divorces is at a similar level.

2 Sometimes Task 1 requires you to write a report about two diagrams. In this case you need to write an opening statement which comments on both sets of data.

1 Which of the statements below is most appropriate for the bar chart?

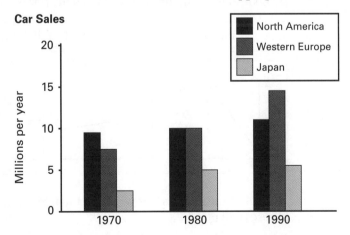

Car Sales

Source: Car Sales from European Business: Texts & Cases.
Butterworth Heinemann. 1994.

A In general car sales have increased since 1970.
B Car sales in North America, Western Europe and Japan are different.

2   Which of the statements below is most appropriate for the line graph?

A   Over 15 million people were using cars in 1990.
B   From 1900 to 1990 the number of car owners dramatically increased.

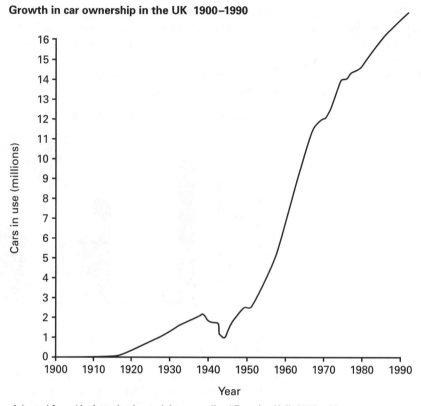

Growth in car ownership in the UK 1900–1990

Adapted from 'An introduction to leisure studies.' Prentice Hall. 2003. p20

3 Now find the best way to combine the two sentences you chose in exercise 2 in an opening statement.

Language focus: Describing change over a period of time

The main aim of Writing Task 1 is to describe information shown in diagrams.

1 Look at the diagrams below. Match the phrases to the appropriate diagram.

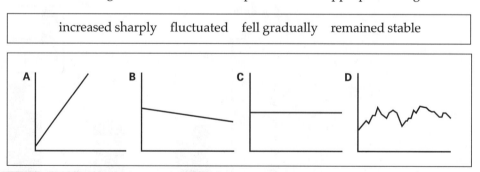

increased sharply   fluctuated   fell gradually   remained stable

2 Look at the phrases below. Match them to the phrases in exercise 1. Not all of the phrases will match.

Example: *sharp increase* – sharp rise

reached a peak   rose dramatically   decreased steadily   varied
stayed the same   increased gradually   fell slightly

3 Read the paragraph below which describes the bar chart. <u>Underline</u> the verbs and say why each tense is used.

The bar chart shows that sales of cars rose most significantly in Western Europe where the number almost doubled from about 7.5 million per year in 1970 to nearly 15 million in 1990. More cars were sold in this area than anywhere else.

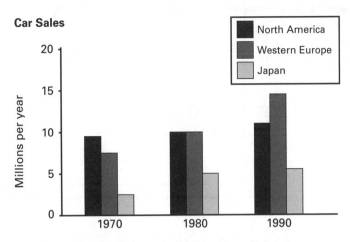

Car Sales

Source: Car Sales from European Business: Texts & Cases. Butterworth Heinemann. 1994.

4 Choose the best alternative from the words in *italics*.

In Japan there was a (1) *same/similar* trend in that sales (2) *doubled/increased two times* between 1970 and 1980 from 2.5 to 5 million. However, over the next ten years the number of cars sold (3) *remained stable/stayed the same*. North America had the (4) *tallest/highest* sales (5) *figures/numbers* in 1970 (about 9 million) but there was only (6) *a little/slight* increase to just over 10 million over the next 20 years.

5 Read the text and complete the gaps with an appropriate word or phrase from the box.

sharp fall   rise   increased   rose steadily   remained stable
increased dramatically

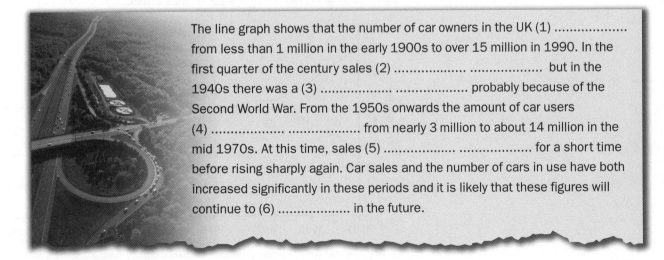

The line graph shows that the number of car owners in the UK (1) .... from less than 1 million in the early 1900s to over 15 million in 1990. In the first quarter of the century sales (2) .... but in the 1940s there was a (3) .... probably because of the Second World War. From the 1950s onwards the amount of car users (4) .... from nearly 3 million to about 14 million in the mid 1970s. At this time, sales (5) .... for a short time before rising sharply again. Car sales and the number of cars in use have both increased significantly in these periods and it is likely that these figures will continue to (6) .... in the future.

6 Look at the line graph below and complete the gaps using an appropriate phrase to describe the changes shown.

Describing change

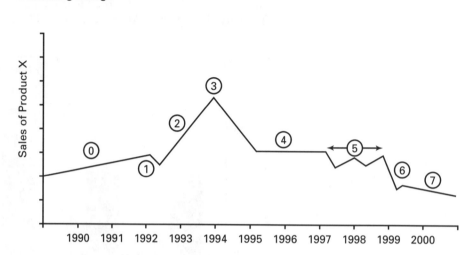

0 A *steady increase/gradual rise* in sales.
  Sales *increased steadily/rose gradually* .
1 A .... in sales.
  Sales ....
2 A .... in sales.
  Sales ....
3 Sales .... in 1993.
4 Sales ....
5 Sales ....
6 A .... in sales.
  Sales ....
7 A .... in sales.
  Sales ....

Skills practice

Study the diagram. Then write four sentences to describe the information shown.

Households with regular use of a car in Great Britain

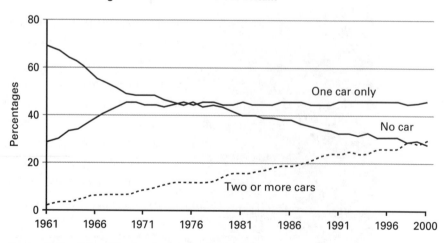

Source: National Travel Survey, Department for Transport

Skills development

Selecting and grouping key information

1 Study the bar charts. Then read the six statements **A–F** below. Choose the three statements that best represent the most important information from the charts.

Most popular sports participated in by young people in England in 1999

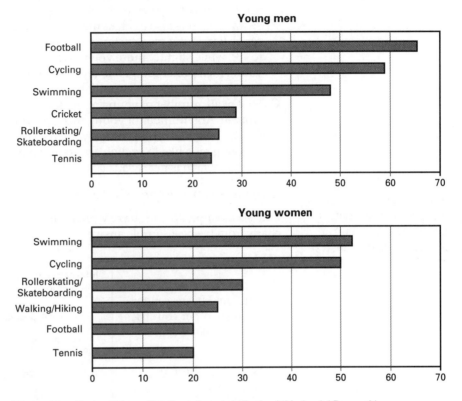

Source: Sport England-Young People and sports in England (Morisocial Research)
Adapted from 'Social Trends' 2002 edition. No 32, p215

A Swimming is the most popular sport for young women.
B The same number of young women (20) said they liked football and tennis.
C Fewer than 30 young men interviewed play cricket.
D Cycling is nearly as popular as swimming for young women.
E Football is the most popular sport for young men.
F Rollerskating/skateboarding are the third most popular sports for young women.

2 Look at the bar charts above again. Read the six statements **A–F** below and choose the three that best show how to group key information from both charts.

A Young men and women both play tennis.
B Cycling and swimming are very popular sports for young men and women.
C 30 young women and 25 young men interviewed participate in rollerskating or skateboarding.
D Playing football is the most popular sport for young men, but is the least popular for young women (with tennis) of those shown on the chart.
E Swimming is more popular with young women than young men, whereas the opposite is true of cycling.
F Cricket is popular with young men, whereas hiking and walking are popular with young women.

3 Now read parts of three sample answers for the bar charts in exercise 1. Which do you think is the best answer and why?

A Football is the most popular sport for young men (64), but the least popular (with tennis) for young women (20). Cycling is the second most popular sport for young men (58) and women (50). Swimming is the third most popular sport for young men (48) and the most popular for young women (52). Tennis is the least most popular sport for young men (23) and women (20).

B The charts clearly show that playing football was the most popular sporting activity for young men (over 60 chose this), whereas young women prefer swimming. It is also evident that cycling and swimming are popular with both sexes. For young men cycling is far more popular than swimming (58 compared to 48), while slightly more young women swim than cycle (52 to 50). Although young men prefer football to any other sport, for young women it was the least popular sporting activity (with tennis) of those shown in the charts.

C First of all, number of young men play football are 3 times more than young women. And number of young men and young woman like to swimming are similar, just around six young woman more than young men. Secondly, number of young men like to cycling are approximate nine young men more than young woman which is nearly 50.

Language focus: Expressing comparison and contrast

Find six examples of language which compares or contrasts the data shown in the charts from the best sample answer.

Remember
Include a range of different expressions to compare or contrast data in your answer.

Skills practice

1 Look at the chart showing statistics for UK passengers travelling to other countries and answer the questions below.

1 What does this bar chart show?
2 What does the vertical axis represent?
3 What does the horizontal axis represent?
4 What do each of the shaded columns represent?
5 What are the most significant features in this diagram?

2 Read and comment on the sample answer below. Consider:
- important information
- length
- style

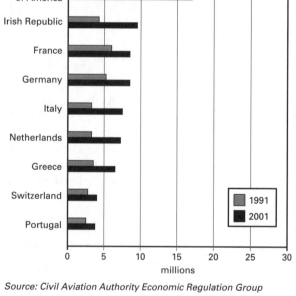

International passenger movements by air from the United Kingdom 1991 and 2001

Source: Civil Aviation Authority Economic Regulation Group

From the bar charts it's easy to see increasing of the international passengers movements by air in 1991 and 2001. Ten countries had been researched and we can see that passenger movements by air are much higher in 2001 than 1991.

Spain passengers occupy the most frequent movements in 1991, the second most frequently movements are taken by USA passengers, the third is by France passengers. By 2001 in some case, the increasing is more than 100% such as Spain, USA and Irish Republic. Also in some countries, it was slight increased such as switzerland and Portugal.

The data also shows that the international passenger movements by air in spain and USA is 3 or 4 times higher than others both in 1991 and 2001. In the ten years, it has been increased a lot.

3 Check and correct the grammar, vocabulary and spelling.

Skills development

Describing a process

Read the statements below. They describe the different stages in the enrolment procedure for a person who wants to do an English course at a language school or college.

- ☐ The student pays the fees for the course.
- ☐ The student's details are put on the computer.
- ☐ The student goes to the institution and completes a placement test.
- ☐ The student has now enrolled and is given a student card.
- ☐ The student is placed in a class at the appropriate level.
- ☐ The student contacts the institution about the English course.
- ☐ The student is interviewed by an experienced teacher.
- ☐ The necessary forms are completed.

1 Which are the first and final stages of this process.

2 Number the sentences in a logical order.

3 <u>Underline</u> the verbs in each sentence. Are they active or passive? Which tenses are used?

4 Choose the best introduction for this enrolment procedure from **A–C**.

A The procedure for this activity is as follows:
B The procedure for improving your English at a language school or college is as follows:
C The procedure for enrolling for an English course at a language school or college is as follows:

5 Choose an appropriate linking word and verb to complete each part of this description of an everyday activity.

| after a few minutes   then   after that   finally   next   ~~first of all~~ |

| add   pour   ~~boil~~   drink   put   take out |

0 ..*first of all boil*.............. the water.

1 .... a teabag into a cup.

2 .... the boiling water into the cup.

3 .... the teabag.

4 .... some milk and sugar and stir.

5 .... the tea.

6 Now add appropriate sequencing words to the sentences in exercise 1 to give the passage more cohesion, eg *first of all, then, finally,* etc.

Skills practice

1 Look at the diagram below about how waste paper is recycled to make better quality paper. Complete the diagram by matching each of the phrases below to a particular stage in the process.

a Package product for distribution to customer

b Pass through heavy roller ⟶ squeeze out water

c Press and flatten into thin sheets

d cut into sheets or rolls

e sort into categories, eg newspapers, computer paper and magazines

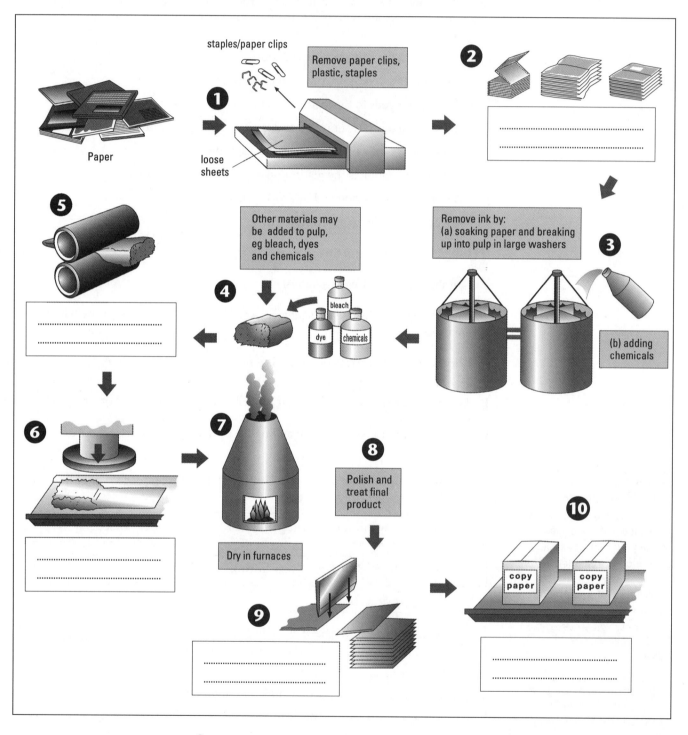

2 Now write a description of the process. Use an appropriate tense, use the passive form where necessary, and add appropriate linking words.

Skills development

Understanding the instructions and the question

IELTS Writing Task 2 questions usually include the following statements:
- You should spend about 40 minutes on this task.
- Present a written argument or case to an educated reader with no specialist knowledge of the following topic.
- Use your own ideas, knowledge and experience and support your arguments with examples and relevant evidence.

1 Decide if these statements are True or False.

A You must spend exactly 40 minutes on this task.
B To write about the topics, you need general rather than specialist knowledge.
C You don't need to include your opinions.
D You should present a clear argument giving examples and reasons.
E Your writing should be in an informal, personal style.

Writing Task 2 questions usually include one of these instructions:
- To what extent do you agree or disagree with this statement?
- Discuss.
- What are your opinions on this?

2 Match the instructions above to these explanations.

A Present both sides of this issue
B Give your personal views on this issue
C How much do you agree or disagree with this issue?

Understanding the topic and the task

Answer these questions.

Settling into a new culture can be extremely difficult. Although some 'culture shock' is inevitable, there are a number of ways to make living overseas much easier. Discuss.

1 What is the main topic?	2 What is the task?
A Visiting foreign countries and new cultures.	**A** Suggest ways to reduce the effects of 'culture shock'.
B The difficulties of studying overseas.	**B** Write about the advantages of living overseas.
C Adapting to life in a new country.	**C** Give reasons why living in the UK is more difficult than living in other countries.

Remember
- Make sure you understand what the topic or subject of the question is. Underline key words if necessary.
- Read the question carefully to identify exactly what you need to do.
- Focus on the question itself, not on what you want to write about.

Skills practice

1 Identify the topics and tasks for these questions.

1 *One of the most serious problems that cities now face is crime. What are the most effective measures to tackle crime in urban areas?*

Main topic:
Task:

2 *The effects of increased global tourism are more likely to be harmful than beneficial. Discuss.*

Main topic:
Task:

3 *Using animals to test the safety of cosmetics or drugs used for medical reasons is never acceptable. To what extent do you agree with this statement?*

Main topic:
Task:

In the IELTS Writing Task 2, candidates will be assessed on their ability to:

i   present the solution to a problem
ii   present and justify an opinion or evaluate and challenge ideas
iii compare and contrast evidence and opinions

2 Find the verbs in statements **i–iii** above that mean:
- to consider how things are different and how they are similar
- to show a good reason for something
- to compare two things to show how they are different
- to question whether something is true or accurate

3 Now match statements **i–iii** to questions **1–3**.

Brainstorming and planning

1 Look at the question about settling into a new culture. Then decide where to put the items in the table. The first one has been done for you as an example.

Settling into a new culture can be extremely difficult. Although some 'culture shock' is inevitable, there are a number of ways to make living overseas much easier. Discuss.

keep in contact with friends/family   people   ~~language~~   culture and lifestyle
accommodation   find out about the place before you go
try and meet/speak to local people   food and drink   religion
join a club or society   sample local food   observe/respect local customs
miss friends/family   ~~learn the language~~

Problems of living overseas	Ways to make living overseas easier
language	learn the language

2 Can you add one more point to each column in the table?

3 Now decide which you think are the three greatest difficulties when settling into a new culture.

4 Look at the three diagrams below. Which is the most appropriate essay structure for a Task 2 answer?

A
Introduction
- - - - - - - - - - - - - - - - - - - -
Main body
- - - - - - - - - - - - - - - - - - - -
Conclusion

B
Introduction
- - - - - - - - - - - - - - - -
Main body
- - - - - - - - - - - - - - - -
Conclusion

C
Introduction
- - - - - - - - - - - - - - - - - -
Main body
- - - - - - - - - - - - - - - - - -
Conclusion

Remember

- A good essay or composition must have a beginning, a middle and an end.
- Decide what you're going to write and make a brief plan outlining what each paragraph will contain.
- Write brief notes on what you want to include in each paragraph. This helps to prompt you as you write your essay and serves as a useful checklist when you have finished.
- A useful guideline to follow is to write an introduction of approximately 50 words, the main body of 170 words or more and a conclusion of 30–40 words. However, these amounts are flexible.

5 Which would be the best overall structure for this question?

Settling into a new culture can be extremely difficult. Although some 'culture shock' is inevitable, there are a number of ways to make living overseas much easier. Discuss.

A
Para. 1 – Intro: main difficulties of living overseas
Para. 2 – Examples of inevitable culture shock
Para. 3 – Suggestions on how to reduce culture shock
Para. 4 – Summary / conclusion of points above

B
Para. 1 – Intro: living and working overseas
Para. 2 – Examples of positive points of living overseas
Para. 3 – Examples of negative points of living overseas
Para. 4 – Summary of your opinion

C
Para. 1 – Intro: why you enjoy living overseas
Para. 2 – Reasons why people live overseas
Para. 3 – Suggestions on best places to live and study overseas

THE INTRODUCTION

Aim and contents

- A good introduction includes a general statement about the topic and says what the purpose of the essay is.
- It may also include the initial views of the writer on this subject – views that will be developed later.
- An introduction must be clear and relevant.

Which of the introductions below is most appropriate for this question. Why?

Settling into a new culture can be extremely difficult. Although some 'culture shock' is inevitable, there are a number of ways to make living overseas much easier. Discuss.

Remember

- Don't copy out the question. You will not gain marks for this.
- The introduction needs to be relevant to the question.
- Write in an impersonal, academic style.

1 *Settling into a new culture can be very difficult. Although some 'culture shock' is inevitable, there are many ways to make living abroad easier.*

2 *I really enjoy living abroad but sometimes it is very hard and I miss my friends and family. I have been living in the UK for two years now and the best thing about it is learning English. However, the weather is awful and I really hate the food!*

3 *People move overseas to live, study or work for many different reasons. Although this can be a very positive experience there will often be difficulties to overcome. These problems might include getting used to living in a different culture, not knowing the language or simply missing friends and family.*

THE MAIN BODY

Aim and contents

- This is the main part of your essay and will develop the key ideas and topic mentioned in the introduction.
- In IELTS Writing Task 2, this section will probably consist of two or three paragraphs.
- This section must be related to the opening and closing paragraphs.

1 Read the question again. Then rearrange the sentences **A–F** below to make a clear paragraph. Consider:

1 Which is the topic sentence (the sentence that gives the main idea of this paragraph)?
2 Which sentences provide supporting evidence for the main idea?
3 Which sentence provides the link with the next paragraph?

Settling into a new culture can be extremely difficult. Although some 'culture shock' is inevitable, there are a number of ways to make living overseas much easier. Discuss.

A Not being able to speak the language very well can make life even more difficult.
B However, there are a number of ways to reduce the difficulties.
C Adjusting to a new culture can often take weeks or months.
D In addition, other problems may arise from different lifestyles, types of food or accommodation.
E During this period it is not uncommon for people to feel very homesick and really miss their friends and family.
F There is no doubt that living overseas can be very difficult at times.

2 Now write the first paragraph of the main body of your answer using sentences **A–F** above.

3 Put the linking words in the box in the appropriate place in the table. Then add one more word for each column.

Sequencers	Reason or result	Contrast	Extra information
firstly	as a result	however	in addition

4 Choose an appropriate linking word from the box to complete the paragraph.

(1) .... , it is a good idea to find as much information as possible before you move to another country by reading books or searching the Internet. (2) .... , speak to other people who have lived abroad and discuss their experiences. (3) .... , it is important to learn the language and (4) .... taking lessons is advisable. When you are living in a new country, if possible, try and make friends with local people (5) .... you do not become lonely or isolated. (6) .... , it is useful to keep in contact with people from your own country too. (7) .... aim to be open-minded about the whole experience.

> **Remember**
> Paragraphs and topic sentences give your writing structure and provide links between sections.

> ~~in addition~~ because
> secondly therefore
> finally besides
> ~~however~~ despite this
> so although ~~firstly~~
> moreover ~~as a result~~

5 What are the four suggestions given in this paragraph about how to reduce 'culture shock'?

6 Improve the information by using an appropriate linking word. The first one has been done for you as an example.

0   The city centre flat was very expensive. A lot of traffic noise could be heard. (*Extra information*)
     The city centre flat was very expensive. In addition/Moreover, a lot of traffic noise could be heard.

Remember
Use linking words to give your writing cohesion

1   Many women have successful careers nowadays. Compared to men, not many women have senior positions. (*Contrast*)
2   In England I live with a host family. My spoken English has improved rapidly. (*Result*)
3   Many students go overseas to study. They believe the quality of education is higher. (*Reason*)

CONCLUSION

Aim and contents

The concluding paragraph sums up the key points covered in the essay.

1 Read the question again and choose the best conclusion for it from **A–C** below. Give your reasons.

Settling into a new culture can be extremely difficult. Although some 'culture shock' is inevitable, there are a number of ways to make living overseas much easier. Discuss.

A   *Last but not least, living abroad is very difficult.*

B   *Although living abroad results in inevitable problems, it is clear that a number of strategies could be useful in preventing many of these difficulties. If this advice is taken, the experience is likely to be far more positive.*

C   *To sum up, here's my advice to you. Try and learn a language, speak to local people and follow local habits and traditions. I'm sure if you do this you'll be fine and everything will be great. That's all.*

Remember
- The conclusion must refer back to the points made in the essay. Don't include new information.
- The conclusion can sum up your views but should be written in an impersonal, academic style.

2 Use the words below to write a different conclusion for this question.

In/conclusion/settling/new/country/cause/problems
Some/difficulties/cannot/avoided/example …
However/there/solutions/such as …
Living/abroad/often/positive/experience/enjoy/possible

....
....
....

Skills practice

1 Do you remember what the topic and the task were for this question?

One of the most serious problems that cities now face is crime. What are the most effective measures to tackle crime in urban areas?

Topic:
Task:

2 Brainstorm ideas for the question above. Use the table to make notes.

Other problems in cities	Crimes	Ways to prevent/reduce
congestion	murder	more police

3 Suggest an outline for the question.

Paragraph 1 ....

Paragraph 2 ....

Paragraph 3 ....

Paragraph 4 ....

Paragraph 5 ....

4 Choose the best topic sentence A, B or C for the introduction below.

A *Crime is a really big problem in all cities.*
B *There is no doubt that numerous problems exist in most modern cities.*
C *Nowadays crime is more important than any other city problem.*

Although traffic congestion, pollution and overcrowding often occur, many people believe that crime is the most serious problem in urban areas. Indeed, television and newspaper reports often tell us that crime continues to rise. However, it is possible to tackle this serious issue in a number of ways.

5 In the first paragraph of the main body, you could say that your first solution to reduce crime would be to increase the number of police. Write a suitable topic sentence below.

....

If more police were on the streets, whether on foot or in patrol cars, criminals would be less likely to commit crimes and people would feel much safer. Having more police visible at night would be particularly beneficial.

6 In the next paragraph, the topic sentence is given. Write two or three supporting sentences.

A second possibility would be to make laws stricter and punishments more severe.

....

....

....

....

....

7 In the next paragraph, number the sentences in the correct order.

☐ *This would reduce burglary and theft.*

☐ *Thirdly, methods to increase security might deter potential criminals.*

☐ *In terms of personal safety, rape alarms or even small weapons could prevent some attacks on people.*

☐ *For example, more effective alarms in houses and cars.*

☐ *In addition, more information about home security would also be useful.*

8 Choose an appropriate word or phrase from the box to complete the gaps in the final paragraph.

> increased do however would are ways reduced although
> in addition methods

In conclusion, (1) .... crime is a major problem in most cities in the world, the situation can be addressed by adopting the (2) .... mentioned above. In this way, the negative effects could be (3) .... and people living in cities (4) .... feel much safer.

Now check the model answer on page 82.

Further practice

You should spend about 40 minutes on this task.

Write about the following topic:

Using animals to test the safety of cosmetics or drugs used for medical reasons is never acceptable. To what extent do you agree with this statement?

Give reasons for your answer and include any examples from your own knowledge or experience.

Write at least 250 words.

Study Skills: Speaking

How much do you know about the IELTS Speaking module?

Do the quiz below to find out.

1 How long is the Speaking module?
   A 15–20 minutes
   B 11–14 minutes
   C 40–45 minutes

2 There are three main parts of the Speaking module. Are these statements about the three Parts true or false?

Part 1

1 This Part lasts between four and five minutes.
2 The candidate is asked to describe a picture.
3 The candidate answers general questions about themselves, their families, their jobs and other familiar topics.

Part 2

4 The candidate is given a minute to prepare to talk about a topic.
5 The candidate is asked to talk about a topic for ten minutes.
6 The candidate must choose what topic they wish to discuss.

Part 3

7 This Part lasts between four and five minutes.
8 This Part is a discussion between the candidate and examiner on a topic related to Part 2
9 This is the easiest Part of the module.

Part 1

Talking about familiar topics

In Part 1 of the Speaking module, you have to answer questions about familiar topics. You can't know exactly what you will be asked, but you can prepare.

Look at the topics below. Write questions that the examiner might ask you about them. Then look at the suggestions on page 83.

- Your studies
- Your previous work experience, your current job or your future career plans
- Your family / home life
- Your country
- Your hobbies and interests

Giving a good answer

1 Read some possible questions and answers for Part 1. Tick the answers that you think are good.

A **Examiner:** Who was your favourite teacher at school? Why did you like their lessons?
Candidate: Mr Wallis. Because they were easy.

B **Examiner:** How long have you been studying English?
Candidate: I am very interested in English because it is a world language and I hope it will help me to do well in my career.

C **Examiner:** What do you do?
Candidate: Well, at the moment I'm studying full time, but back in my country I'm a doctor and I hope to be able to find work here as a doctor too.

D **Examiner:** What are the best things about your job?
Candidate: Oh, definitely the people. I love meeting people from all over the world.

E **Examiner:** Do you live with your family?
Candidate: No.

F **Examiner:** How long have you been in the UK?
Candidate: I will stay three years.

G **Examiner:** Tell me about where you are living at the moment.
Candidate: It is a, er, er, what is the word, er, er, maisonette!

H **Examiner:** Do you enjoy travelling?
Candidate: Yes, I'm really interested in seeing the world. While I've been living in Britain, I've also taken the opportunity to go to Europe and see France and Spain. I found the people in Spain really friendly.

---

2 How can you improve the other answers?

3 Now record yourself answering the same questions. Listen to the recording and evaluate your performance.

Useful language

At the moment I'm living/studying/working …
Before that I lived in …
Recently, I've been to France/started playing football, etc.
(*note the use of the present perfect here*)
I'm planning to …
After that I'll probably …

I prefer (*followed by a noun*) Scotland because …
I'd rather (*followed by verb*) live in Australia because …

Both my father and mother …
Neither of my brothers …
None of my friends …

It depends. Sometimes I like cooking, and sometimes I'm just too tired.
Definitely, I love it! It's …
Mmm, possibly. It depends on the weather really.
Generally I think it's a good idea because …
Well, it's very different because …

Let me think/see, …
I'm not really sure, but perhaps …
That's a good question/point. I suppose …
I haven't really given that much thought before but …

---

4 Write answers that are true for you to the questions below.

1 Why are you taking IELTS?
2 What are your ambitions?
3 Tell me about where you are living at the moment.
4 How would you describe your home town?
5 What do you usually do at the weekend?

Identifying strengths and weaknesses

Remember
- Make sure you answer the question.
- One-word answers are not acceptable.
- Always add some extra information to your answer.

1 🗎 23 Listen to a student answering the examiner's questions. What is good about their performance? How could it be improved? Use the checklist to help you and refer to the Recording script on page 93.

Checklist
- Does the student answer the questions correctly?
- Does she answer the questions fully, giving extra information?
- Is her grammar accurate?
- Does she use a range of vocabulary appropriately?
- Is it easy to understand her pronunciation?
- Does she use any words or phrases to make her language sound more natural, eg *Well, Actually, Oh definitely*, etc.?
- Does she sound fluent or does she often hesitate?

---

2 Now record yourself answering the same questions (see page 93 for the questions). Listen to the recording and evaluate your performance using the checklist above.

Planning your answer

In Part 2 of the Speaking module you have to speak for 1–2 minutes on a topic. You have one minute to think about this topic. Use this time well.

1 Read the sample question below. <u>Underline</u> the key words in the instructions.

> Describe an occasion when you have been successful. You should say:
> • where and when you were successful
> • how you were successful
> • what you had to do to make sure you were successful
> and describe how you felt about your success.

2 Think of two or three things to say about each part of the question. You can make notes if you wish, but remember you only have **one** minute.

Giving extra information

It is important that you talk for long enough: minimum one minute and maximum two minutes. This means you have to think of extra information to give the examiner. You can do this in different ways by:
• saying why you think/feel something
• giving examples
• giving details

1 Read this sample question and <u>underline</u> the key words.

> Talk about an important day in your life. You should say:
> • when this day was
> • if you were alone or with others
> • where you were and what happened
> and explain why this day was important to you.

2 Think of relevant things to say about each part of the question. Give examples and include details.

3 Use the different parts of the question to organize your answer, so that each part follows on logically from the one before.

4 🔲 24 Now listen to this student answering the question. Does he include all of the main points?

> **Remember**
> It is important to keep talking, but don't talk about things which are not related to the topic.

5 Look at the *Useful language* box and practise answering the two sample questions. Time yourself to check your answers are the right length.

Describe a present someone gave you which was/is important to you.
You should say:
- what the present was
- who gave it to you
- why they gave it to you (eg to celebrate a birthday)
and explain why it is so important to you.

Describe a friend who has played an important part in your life. You should say:
- how you met this person
- how long you have known them
- the kind of things you do or did with them
and explain why they have been important in your life.

Identifying strengths and weaknesses

📼 **25** Listen to answers to the second sample question. Which one is a better answer? Why?

Follow-up questions

After you have spoken for 1–2 minutes, the examiner may ask you one or two follow-up questions about what you have said. For example:

Question	Answer	Follow-up question
How did you feel when you arrived in the UK?	I was very nervous because I didn't know anybody.	Did you find it easy to meet people?

1 Match the appropriate answers **A–F** to questions **1–6**.

1 Do you enjoy playing sports?
2 Would you like to go there again?
3 Do you think it will be easy to get a job in IT?
4 Have you ever been to any other countries in Europe?
5 Would you consider doing the same sort of job again?
6 Would you recommend the holiday to other people?

A No, not really. It wasn't very good value for money.
B I don't think so. It wasn't really for me.
C I expect so. It's a growing industry.
D Yes, definitely. I particularly enjoy outdoor ones.
E Possibly. It would depend on who I went with!
F Yes, a few. France, Spain and the Czech Republic.

2 📼 **26** Listen and check.

3 📼 **26** Listen again and repeat the answers.

Part 3

Remember
- One-word answers are **not** acceptable.
- Always give a reason for your answer.

Expanding answers

In Part 3 of the Speaking module, you have to discuss questions related to the topic in Part 2 with the examiner. Although this is a discussion, you should do most of the talking. Sometimes the examiner will ask you questions which seem to need a one word answer. For example:

1 Is it a good idea to exercise regularly?
2 Is there more crime these days?
3 Do you think everyone should have a mobile phone?

1 Read the example questions above again. Write an answer for each including a reason.

2 Now add an extra sentence or two to each of your answers.

Linking ideas

1 The words and phrases in the box are all used to link ideas. Put them into the appropriate categories below.

| on the other hand | and | so | because | however | such as |

1 the reason for something
2 the result of something
3 joining two ideas together

4 contrasting two ideas
5 giving an example

2 Look at the *Useful language* boxes and practise giving answers to questions **1–8** below.

> **Remember**
> Some linking words, such as *furthermore, nevertheless* and *consequently* are more appropriate for writing than speaking.

Useful language: Comparing and contrasting

On the one hand … on the other hand …
Well, … isn't as … as …
… is nowhere near as … as …

I'd rather …
I'd much prefer (to) …

It depends (on) …

Useful language: Making predictions/talking about the future

There's a good chance that …
I doubt very much if …

I hope that …
I expect that …
I'm afraid that … (*this does not mean you feel fear, but is a way of talking about something negative, eg I'm afraid that a lot of smokers will complain, but …*)
It's bound to (+ *infinitive*)

It is/isn't very likely to …

Useful language: Giving opinions

As far as I'm concerned …
It seems to me that …
I can't help thinking that … (*use this phrase when you think that people won't agree with you*)
I tend to think that …

---

1 Do you think smoking will be banned in all public places?
2 Do you prefer to go out or stay at home in the evening?
3 Do you think that email has made our lives easier?
4 Which is better: living in the countryside or in the city?
5 Are qualifications important?
6 How likely is it that computers will be able to do your job in future?
7 Would you rather watch sport or play it?
8 What do you think the consequences of global warming will be?

---

3 🖭 27 Now listen to students answering the eight questions above.

- Do they give full answers?
- Do they use a range of vocabulary?
- Are their answers grammatically correct?

Section 1   Questions 1–10

Questions 1 and 2

Circle the appropriate letter.

1   Where does the man study?
  A   Aston University
  B   William's University
  C   Birmingham University
  D   Edgbaston University

2   What kind of property does the man want?
  A   a three bedroom flat
  B   a two bedroom property
  C   a one bedroom house with a garden
  D   a property with a garage

Questions 3–6

Complete the table. Write **NO MORE THAN THREE WORDS OR A NUMBER** for each answer.

	Flat 1	Flat 2
Location	Edgbaston	(3) ....
Floor	ground floor	(4) ....
Furnished?	(5)	fully furnished
Price	£480 pcm	(6) .... pcm

Question 7

Circle the appropriate letter.

7   Which of the following are included in the rent?

A   gas
B   water rates
C   electricity
D   phone

Questions 8–10

Complete the notes.

Property address:
(8) ....
Name of client: *John Taylor*
Contact phone number:
(9) *0791* ....
Meet at: (10) .... *p.m.*

Questions 11–15

Complete the summary. Write **NO MORE THAN THREE WORDS** for each answer.

Dangers at the beach in Sydney

Shark attacks are not very common, about (11) ....
take place each year, and box jellyfish are only a problem further
(12) .... Another danger at the beach is
(13) .... , and you should slip on a shirt, slap on a
(14) .... and slop on some sun cream. Far less
(15) .... are rip currents which you are more likely to
die from than anything else.

Questions 16–18

Complete the labels on the diagram. Write **NO MORE THAN THREE WORDS**
for each answer.

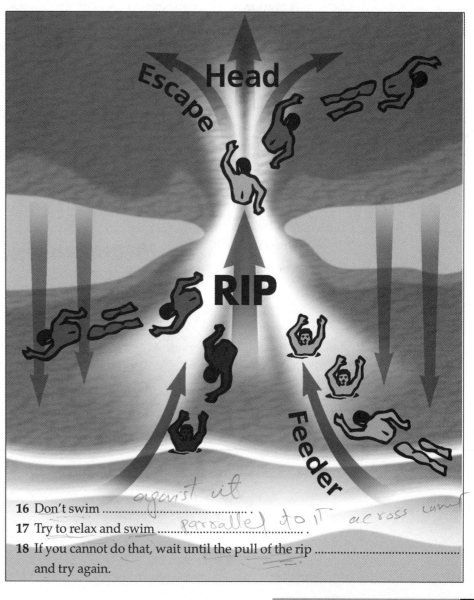

16 Don't swim .... *against it*
17 Try to relax and swim .... *parallel to it across curr*
18 If you cannot do that, wait until the pull of the rip ....
   and try again.

Questions 19 and 20

Complete the sentences. Write **NO MORE THAN THREE WORDS** for each answer.

19 To be safe in the ocean, don't ....

20 Only swim in places where you can see ....

Section 3   Questions 21–30

Questions 21–24

Answer the questions. Write **NO MORE THAN THREE WORDS** for each answer.

21 What subject is Andrew studying?
22 Name the crop that Andrew mentions.
23 Which disadvantage of using chemicals does Andrew mention?
24 Why might insects be beneficial to the farmer?

Questions 25–27

Circle **THREE** appropriate letters **A–F**.

Insects which are beneficial to crop plants are:

A butterflies
B snails
C beetles
D wasps
E caterpillars
F slugs

Questions 28–30

Complete the summary. Write **NO MORE THAN THREE WORDS** for each answer.

A ring of insecticide is **(28)** .... around the tree trunk,

and then the tree is sprayed with a chemical called *pyrethrum*, made from

(29) .... The insects drop from the tree, and the only

the ones with **(30)** .... are able to return safely.

Section 4   Questions 31–40

Questions 31–35

Complete the sentences. Write **NO MORE THAN THREE WORDS OR A NUMBER** for each answer.

31 Two kinds of ownership are mentioned: a sole proprietorship and a

....

32 A corporation has the same legal rights as a ....

33 A board can be as small as ....

34 Shareholders meet .... to vote for the people on the board.

35 The board is like the human brain because they ....

Questions 36–39

Complete the flow chart.
Write **NO MORE THAN THREE WORDS OR A NUMBER** for each answer.

How a corporation works

A business idea is generated

(36) .... is needed

A corporation is formed

(37) .... are sold to raise revenue

Money is invested in equipment and (38) ....

Company makes (39) ....

Dividend paid to shareholders

Question 40

Circle the appropriate letter.

40 Another advantage of a corporation is that
    A you can't go out of business.
    B you can't lose everything you own.
    C you can get sued.
    D you and the restaurant are legally the same.

Reading

Reading Passage 1

You should spend about 20 minutes on **Questions 1–12**, which are based on Reading Passage 1 below.

Emmeline Pankhurst was born in Manchester in 1858 to Robert Goulden, a successful businessman who was also a committed socialist, and Sophia Crane, an ardent feminist. Together with her daughters, Sylvia and Christabel, she is remembered as one of the major figures in the fight for women's suffrage. Although the suffrage movement had been active for at least thirty years, it was her founding of the Women's Social and Political Union (WSPU or *The Union*) in 1903 that really fired the public's imagination, and made 'Votes for Women' the subject of the day.

The small group began with peaceful protests. However, convinced that such methods would not bring the desired result, Christabel and Emmeline decided that a more militant approach was needed to force the government to take notice of their demands. The motto of the WSPU was 'deeds not words'. These militant campaigners became known as *suffragettes*.

On October 13th, 1905, the day before a General Election, Christabel and another WSPU member disrupted a Liberal Party meeting in Manchester by asking 'Will the Liberal Government, if returned, give votes to women?' The question was not answered, so it was repeated by the women who were then summarily ejected from the meeting by the police, who charged them with obstruction, ordering them to pay a fine or face imprisonment. Emmeline offered to pay the fines, but Christabel refused, preferring to go to prison for the cause. Her pioneering action brought a good deal of publicity to the movement, encouraging more women to join their ranks.

On February 19th 1906, the day of the King's speech to Parliament, the WSPU organized a gathering in the capital. Emmeline was due to address a group of suffragettes. When she heard that votes for women had not been even mentioned in the King's speech, she called upon the women to march to the House of Commons, to argue their case. This was the first of many such marches. On the same day the following year, another march resulted in fifty-four women being arrested.

Over the next nine years many more women went to prison for the cause. Once there, they often went on hunger strike, refusing food until they were released. Emmeline and Sylvia were imprisoned many times, and endured hunger strikes. Emmeline went on ten hunger strikes during one eighteen month period alone.

In September 1909, the government introduced the forcible feeding of imprisoned suffragettes who went on hunger strike. Emmeline's response to this clearly shows her passion. `The spirit which is in woman today', she warned, `cannot be quenched; it is stronger than all earthly potentates and powers, than all tyranny, cruelty and oppression'.

By 1911, as a deputation marched to Parliament, a smaller group of women armed with stones and hammers broke the windows of government buildings. This was a sign of things to come. In the remaining years before the Great War, the WSPU became increasingly violent, something that Sylvia was unhappy about, preferring a peaceful approach. On March 1st 1912, Emmeline and two other WSPU members smashed windows at 10 Downing Street, while 150 other suffragettes broke shop windows in London's West End. Up to this point, the WSPU had given advance warning of its militant demonstrations, but this attack came out of the blue. Emmeline was sentenced to two months' imprisonment and Christabel was forced to go into temporary exile in France, not returning until war broke out in 1914.

Sylvia finally left the WSPU in 1912 when the Union adopted a policy of widespread arson. She was also frustrated by her sister's attempts to gain middle class support by abandoning the fight for universal adult suffrage in favour of limited suffrage for only middle class women.

When war was declared, the WSPU called a truce and Emmeline and Christabel committed themselves to supporting the war effort. As a pacifist, however, Sylvia set up the Women's Peace Army, an organization devoted to securing a negotiated settlement. After the War it quickly became clear that women, or at least middle class women, would soon get the vote. The wartime roles they had taken on outside the home as nurses, factory workers and so on had gone a long way towards convincing the Government of their fitness to use the franchise wisely. As a result, the WSPU turned itself into a formal political party, aiming to enter Parliament and was renamed the Women's Party in November 1917.

In February 1918, women over the age of thirty were finally given the vote provided that they were either householders, married to householders, occupied property with an annual rent of 5 [pounds sterling] or more, or graduates of a British university. Emmeline was determined that Christabel should be the first woman MP, and having campaigned enthusiastically for her, was bitterly disappointed when her daughter failed to win a seat in Parliament.

While Sylvia remained a committed socialist, her sister and mother were moving further towards the right, with Emmeline joining the Conservative party in 1925 and standing as a candidate for election. Sylvia was appalled. When Emmeline Pankhurst died on June 14th 1928, she was still estranged from her daughter Sylvia. She died just a few weeks before British women were given voting rights equal to those of men.

Despite their increasingly different agendas, all three Pankhurst women were important in the fight for British women's suffrage, and women across the world owe much to their efforts, and to the efforts of their fellow campaigners. Nonetheless, it must be recognized that the acceptance of women's suffrage may also have been due to changing attitudes towards the role and capabilities of women, brought on in part by their efforts during the First World War.

Questions 1–5

Classify the following descriptions as referring to

Emmeline Pankhurst   **E**

Christabel Pankhurst   **C**

Sylvia Pankhurt   **S**

1   .... was the first Pankhurst to go to prison for the cause.

2   .... preferred a non-violent approach to campaigning.

3   .... attempted to be the first female Member of Parliament.

4   .... did not stand as a candidate for election.

5   .... did not live to see the day when all British women were given the right to vote.

Questions 6–10

Do the following statements agree with the information given in Reading Passage 1?
Write:

YES	if the statement agrees with the information
NO	if the statement contradicts the information
NOT GIVEN	if there is no information on this

6 Emmeline Pankhurst started the campaign for women's suffrage.
7 The word 'suffragette' describes everyone who was in favour of women's suffrage.
8 Over 50 women were arrested after a march to Parliament in February 1907.
9 While in exile in France, Christabel continued to organize protests back in Britain.
10 Sylvia left the WSPU before the Great War broke out.

Questions 11 and 12

Circle the appropriate letter.

11 According to the writer, the Pankhursts
    A are internationally famous to this day.
    B are largely responsible for British women gaining the vote.
    C helped the British to win the First World War.
    D are part of the reason why British women were given the vote.

12 A suitable title for this passage would be:
    A A history of the WSPU
    B Three key figures in the fight for women's suffrage
    C A political history of the early twentieth century
    D Great women of the twentieth century

Reading Passage 2

You should spend about 20 minutes on **Questions 13–25**, which are based on Reading Passage 2 below.

Every day for the last few months, the forests of Portugal and southern Spain have echoed with the sound of chopping wood as gangs of cork strippers bring this year's harvest to a close. This corner of Western Europe provides 80 per cent of the world's cork, and the traditional methods used to strip it have barely changed. With a special axe called a *machado*, a cork stripper makes a series of neat vertical cuts in the trunk, taking care not to swing too deep and kill the tree. The two-inch-thick bark is then gently prised away, leaving the tree naked from the waist down, with its upper branches untouched. Slowly the bark grows back, and after nine years the whole process begins again. The harvested cork is used in everything from gasketing materials to shoe soles, but its primary role has always been keeping wine and air apart. It is wine producers who provide the cork farmers with the majority of their income. In 1999, according to government figures, bottle stoppers accounted for 71 per cent of cork exports by value. And as the world's biggest producer, the Portuguese cork industry is vital to the country's economy, earning 740 million euro in foreign sales last year and employing an estimated 500,000 people.

Since the first factories began punching corks 200 years ago, the cork and wine trades have gone hand in hand. But lately the relationship has been showing signs of strain, especially in the UK where supermarkets are losing patience with natural cork's occasional imperfections. They claim the level of cork-taint, caused by a rogue chemical compound known as TCA, is unacceptable, and are moving swiftly towards synthetic stoppers. And this could spell the end for the cork forests of Portugal.

The first reliable plastic cork was invented in 1992 by the American company Supremecorq, which now supplies over 400 wineries worldwide. Today, its patented 'thermoplastic stopper' is being chased by seven plastic look-a-likes in the race to plug the 15 billion wine bottles produced each year. So far, plastic manufacturers have an estimated 2 per cent of the total, but this is set to rise exponentially. The only barrier, as they see it, is a vague, sentimental attachment among consumers towards natural cork. In the UK, having convinced the big buyers who control 75 per cent of the market, this is beginning to erode fast. Already a quarter of the wines sold by Tesco and Asda/Walmart are bottled under plastic, and their main rivals are not far behind. Having spent the last 20 years studying the cork forests, wildlife biologist Dr Luis Palma is in no doubt about the threat to the environment if cork loses the battle against plastic, for Portugal's 720,000 hectares of cork forests – a third of the world's total – support a fragile, biodiverse ecosystem. 'The value of the forests will diminish and there will be irresistible economic pressure for them to be replaced,' he says. 'It is hard to see anything that could replace cork that would be environmentally sustainable given the poor soil and harsh climate.' And the forests also support other aspects of the local economy. 'On a small patch of cork land a farmer can raise a herd of goats, a few cows and some pigs to forage for acorns and graze beneath the trees,' explains Helena Freitas, President of Portugal's oldest conservation group, the *Liga para a Proteccao da Natureza*.

So are there any alternatives? A Portuguese government scheme to convert the land to cereals after the war to provide food for people and livestock was abandoned as a disaster when it was realised the soil was simply not strong enough to support this type of monoculture. At present, cork's most serious rival is eucalyptus, a fast-growing cash-crop for the paper industry whose total plantings have tripled since the seventies to just under 700,000 hectares. Eucalyptus acts like a sponge, choking off the water supply to other plants, leaving the ground between the trees barren. The Royal Society for the Protection of Birds is deeply concerned about the consequences for a variety of native species and migrating birds such as the Blackcap and Common Crane. And there's also the risk of serious soil erosion leading to possible desertification.

Back in the UK the debate over cork has grown increasingly bitter with some supermarkets claiming that up to one bottle in every 12 is corked, a figure vehemently denied by the cork industry. While millions of pounds are being spent on trying to stamp out TCA, the producers of plastic corks say they just want a share of the market and are not out to replace anyone. But that may not be the way it turns out.

Question 13

Which illustration shows the traditional method of stripping cork?
Choose the correct letter **A–C**.

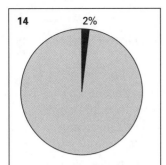

14   2%

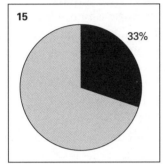

15   33%

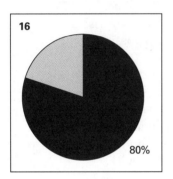

16   80%

Questions 14–16

Label the pie charts. Choose your labels from the box below.

> **A** Percentage of wine bottle-stopper market held by plastic manufacturers
> **B** Percentage of world's wine bottles produced by Spain and Portugal each year
> **C** Percentage of world's cork produced by Portugal and Spain
> **D** Percentage of Portuguese cork used to make wine bottle stoppers
> **E** Percentage of wines sold by Tesco and Asda/Walmart supermarkets that use plastic stoppers
> **F** Percentage of world's cork forests in Portugal
> **G** Percentage of world's eucalyptus grown in Portugal

Questions 17–21

Complete the sentences with words from Reading Passage 2. Write **NO MORE THAN THREE WORDS OR A NUMBER** for each answer.

17 Protecting wine from the air has always been the .... of cork.

18 The cork industry in Portugal is essential to ....

19 Supermarkets prefer plastic stoppers because they say the amount of cork taint is ....

20 Apart from Supremecorq, there are .... other companies making plastic corks.

21 Dr Palma believes that because of the poor soil and harsh climate in Portugal, it would be difficult to find an .... replacement for cork.

Questions 22–24

Complete the table below using information from Reading Passage 2. Write **NO MORE THAN THREE WORDS** for each answer.

Possible alternative crops to cork	Main use of crop	Problems associated with these alternatives
(22)	foodstuffs for people and animals	soil not strong enough
eucalyptus	(23)	soaks up all the (24) ....

Question 25

Circle the appropriate letter.

25 A suitable title for this passage would be
   A Alternative uses for cork
   B Cork forests under threat
   C Eucalyptus or plastic – which is better?
   D Nature in the cork forests

Reading Passage 3

You should spend about 20 minutes on **Questions 26–40**, which are based on Reading Passage 3 below.

A Love, as we all know, hurts. You get the love bug, then love sick, and then your heart breaks. Our very language reflects the emotional links we make between our relationships and our state of health. But researchers now have evidence that the link is more than poetic fancy. The state of our relationship actually does affect our physical health – and not just because of the sleeplessness and poor diet that unhappiness brings. The link is so strong that it affects how rapidly our wounds heal and how well we fight off disease.

B For over 20 years Dr Janice Kiecolt-Glaser and Dr Ronald Glaser, a husband and wife team from Ohio State University, have studied the ways in which stress affects our bodies. In their most recent study the Glasers, a psychologist and immunologist respectively, have found that the way couples deal with conflict has an important effect on their physical well being.

C The researchers looked at 90 couples in their first year of marriage: newly weds were encouraged to discuss subjects known to be a source of disagreement to them – the in-laws, whether to have a baby, money, working late. During the often heated discussions, the couples were videotaped and their arguments were given scores for aggressive or negative behaviour. They also had their blood tested throughout to measure stress hormone levels and immune system activity. Wound healing was also monitored (using equipment attached to specially created blisters on their arms).

D Negative behaviour during arguments, particularly criticism, sarcasm and put downs, resulted in a weakened immune response (measured in activity of one type of white blood cell, T lymphocytes, which works to attack viruses), as well as increased levels of the stress hormones adrenalin, noradrenalin, cortisol and adrenocorticotropic hormone (ACTH) – substances that can further reduce immunity. The researchers also found that in the blisters on the couples' arms, concentrations of compounds called *cytokines* and cells called *neutrophils*, which aid healing and fight infection, were lower in couples who argued aggressively. Measurements over time showed that they healed slower.

E The researchers say that these physical changes brought on by conflict in a relationship may make people susceptible to illness, particularly infectious diseases, perhaps even cancer. The Glasers' earlier work had shown that in people whose immune response was impaired by stress, there was a greater chance that the anti flu jabs and other vaccinations wouldn't work. The effects are not short term. The Glasers followed up their couples ten years later to see how their marriages had fared. Most of those who had argued negatively and who had shown high levels of stress hormones were separated or dissatisfied with their marriages.

F At the most superficial level, the research may explain why our lives generally seem to be falling apart when our relationships are going badly – on a physical level we become less able to cope. But its real importance is that it adds authority to a growing body of research showing that the everyday stresses that we experience from our work and relationships have a direct, rather than merely indirect, impact on our health. An influential study published in the *British Medical Journal* a few years ago, for example, found that depression, anxiety and lack of social support (of the type provided by a secure relationship) all appeared to contribute to coronary heart disease. But dozens of other articles published in the past decade have also provided evidence that unhappy marriages have a negative effect on the circulatory, hormonal, immune and nervous systems. Predictably, a study found that the risk of mental illness increased tenfold when there was mental discord. But studies have also found a link with tooth decay, rheumatoid arthritis and blood pressure. On average, married people – whether happy or unhappy – enjoy better mental and physical health than the unmarried, and women in particular seem to benefit from a good quality marriage. One 15-year study has indicated that, for women, companionship in marriage and equality in decision making were associated with a lower risk of death.

G The lesson for all of us is that once you find love, you should make sure that you respond to the inevitable conflicts constructively and not aggressively – the consequences could be physical as well as emotional.

Questions 26–29

Reading Passage 3 has seven paragraphs **A–G**. Which paragraphs concentrate on the following information?

NB You need only write **ONE** letter for each answer.

Example
How the Glasers' previous work and the follow-up they did later related to this study.   **E**

26 Other research that has found a link between an unhappy marriage and poor health.
27 How the Glasers' research was carried out.
28 The writer's reaction to the results of the research.
29 The evidence the Glasers found for their conclusions.

Questions 30–32

Look at the descriptions of some findings mentioned in Reading Passage 3. Match the findings **A–F** in the box below with the descriptions.

NB There are more findings than descriptions, so you will not use them all.

Example A recent finding of the Glasers   **E**

30 A previous finding of the Glasers ....
31 A finding of an important study published in the *British Medical Journal* ....
32 A finding of another study ....

> **A** Not having a good relationship could be a factor in developing heart disease.
> **B** For both men and women, being happily married means you are less likely to die.
> **C** An unhappy marriage could lead to tooth decay.
> **D** Couples who argue are less successful at work.
> **E** Conflict in a relationship may make people more likely to get ill.
> **F** Stress can affect the immune system to such an extent that vaccinations against illness may not work.

Questions 33–36

Answer the questions. Write **NO MORE THAN THREE WORDS** for each answer.

33 How long have the Glasers been studying the effects of stress?
34 According to the Glasers, what sort of behaviour during arguments can make us more unhealthy?
35 What did the Glasers measure by creating blisters on the arms of the couples they looked at?
36 When did the Glasers study the couples' marriages again?

Questions 37–40

Complete the summary. Choose your answers from the box.

NB There are more answers than spaces so you will not use them all.

> creating   disagree   measuring   respond   conflict   love   heal   physical
> decay   positive   recent   grow   exercise

Through **(37)** .... immune responses, levels of stress hormones and

compounds which help the body to **(38)** .... , the Glasers have found that

how couples deal with **(39)** .... directly affects their health. This agrees

with other research showing that stress has **(40)** .... consequences.

Writing Task 1

You should spend about 20 minutes on this task.

The graph below shows cinema attendance by age in Great Britain.
Write a report for a university lecturer describing the information shown.

Summarize the information by selecting and reporting the main features, and make comparisons where relevant.

Write at least 150 words.

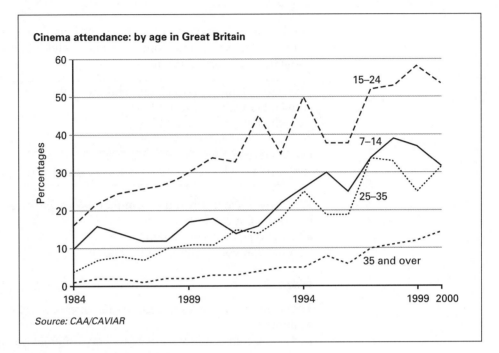

Cinema attendance: by age in Great Britain

Source: CAA/CAVIAR

Writing Task 2

You should spend about 40 minutes on this task.

Write about the following topic:

It is almost impossible for women to have a successful career as well as having the full responsibility of raising a family.
Discuss.

Give reasons for your answer and include any examples from your own knowledge or experience.

Write at least 250 words.

Part 1

The examiner asks you some general questions about yourself, your home, your job or your studies. For example:

- Do you enjoy living here?
- What are the best things about your country?
- Tell me about your family.
- What are your hobbies?

Part 2

The examiner gives you a card with questions similar to those below. You have one minute to think about the topic and make notes if you wish. You should then talk about the topic for 1–2 minutes.

Describe a happy event in your childhood that you remember well. You should say:
- when the event took place
- where the event took place
- what happened exactly

and explain why you remember this event clearly.

When you have finished the examiner, asks a few brief questions about what you have said. For example:
- Did you ever do this again?
- What did your parents think about it?

Part 3

The examiner will ask some discussion questions related to the same topic. For example:
- Do you think children's lives are very different nowadays?
- Are children too protected now?
- Do you think children can have too many toys?
- Is it important to celebrate birthdays and other festivals?

Key for Listening module

Quiz p. 7

1 **B** The Listening module is about 40 minutes long – 30 minutes of listening and 10 minutes at the end to transfer your answers to the answer sheet.
2 **A** There are four Sections.
3 **C** There are 40 questions which may include multiple choice, short answers, filling in charts / diagrams / tables, sentence completion, matching and classifying.
4 True. The texts and questions get more difficult with each Section.
5 True. All the sections are worth the same number of marks, even though the exam gets more difficult.
6 Adam ... **C**   1**C**
  Professor Jones ... **A**   2**B**
  Steve, Mary and Sarah ... **D**   3**D**
  Mr Green ... **B**   4**A**
7 ONCE.
8 Yes. Before each Section, you have about 30 seconds to read the questions for that section.
9 On the question paper, and then transfer them at the end to the answer sheet.
10 True.

Prediction p. 7

1 From the questions, you can predict that a girl, who is probably new to a place, is asking directions from someone. You'll need to listen for a time such as *a week ago* for question 1. As there are several doors to choose from in question 3, she could be looking for an office or a classroom.
2 1 **A**: 'I only arrived here yesterday'
  2 **C**: 'The one with the glass front'
  3 **C**: '… and it's the second door on the left?'

Recognizing repetition and avoiding distracters p. 8

1 Keiko repeats the directions back to Stephan for confirmation.
2 In the last extract, Stephan replied 'That's right!' He means, 'You are correct', but if you are not listening carefully, you might think that the <u>door</u> is on the right.

Completing notes p. 8

1 1 think carefully
  2 near (to) home
  3 study abroad / overseas

3 1 *$130*: 'That's $130 per week, or $90 without meals.' $90 is incorrect because this is the price without meals.

2 *college halls/halls of residence/college residential block*: 'There are three kinds of accommodation that we deal with – home stays, college halls of residence, or private lets.' The instructions do not state that you should use words from the text, so you can use your own, and in this case, you have to as *college halls of residence* is four words and would be incorrect. *College halls residence* is also incorrect as it is ungrammatical.
3 *reasonably priced/fairly priced*: '… but we make sure that you are paying a reasonable price.' You need to change the words from the text to make grammatical sense.

5 4 Jenkins
  5 British
  6 562, Green Park Road
  7 07785 265 981

Listening for numbers and letters p. 9

4 1 *Sir Anthony Winton*. Make sure you can spell *Mr, Mrs, Miss, Ms* and *Sir*.
  2 *34.92*. Numbers after the decimal point are always said individually, eg *point nine two*, not *point ninety-two*.
  3 *15 Sparrow Lane*. Make sure you can spell words like *Lane*.
  4 *29,030* (feet)
  5 *Michael MacWilliams*. There is another capital letter after *Mc* or *Mac*.
  6 *286 Banbury Road*. Abbreviations for *road* (Rd) and *street* (St) are acceptable.
  7 *74%*
  8 *Janet Gates*
  9 *0121 6749544*. All numbers are said separately, except for *double 4*, and there is a pause between each set of numbers.
  10 *654/120084* (/ is usually pronounced *forward slash*)
  11 *Mrs J Robson-Smith*. If someone has two surnames, there is a hyphen between them.
  12 *Flat 3, 547 Oxford Road*
  13 *www. bht.co.uk* (. is pronounced *dot* in web addresses)
  14 *Dr. Brown*
  15 N 770 CES. Numbers are pronounced separately for ID / registration numbers.

Skills practice p. 10

1 C
2 D
3 set menu / three course meal
4 vegetarian / made without meat
5 coffee / cappuccino or espresso
6 12
7 £25
8 (Mr) (Dan) Glover
9 01452 863092

Using key words for prediction p. 11

1 1 A gives information about used car sales. (eg second-hand cars)
   B tells you the best way to buy a car. (eg most efficient / most effective)
   C tells you the most popular way to sell a car. (Note that this is talking about selling, while the others mention buying a car.)
   D looks at different ways of buying a new car. (This answer is the only one that specifies new cars.)

   2 A You are a new driver. (eg you have just passed your test)
   B You have had an accident in your old car. (Listen for words like crash or smash.)
   C You don't have a lot of money. (Listen for cheap or inexpensive.)
   D Your old car is unreliable. (Maybe it often breaks down.)
   E You want to learn to drive. (eg you want driving lessons)

   3 A they have a lot of room to show you the cars. (eg there is a lot of space)
   B they are cheap. (or inexpensive)
   C you have a legal right to return the car if something goes wrong. (eg a warranty / guarantee)
   D they are honest. (eg they are trustworthy / they won't cheat you)

2 and Eliminating wrong answers p. 11

   1 A CORRECT. 'Today we're going to talk about the different ways there are of buying a used car ...'
   B INCORRECT. Not 'the best way' but 'the different ways' of buying a car.
   C INCORRECT. The recording specifies 'of *buying* a used car.'
   D INCORRECT. The recording talks about used cars, not new cars.

   2 A CORRECT. The recording says, '... maybe you've just passed your test ...'
   B INCORRECT. Nothing is mentioned about an accident.
   C CORRECT. The recording says, 'You look at new cars but they are so expensive ...'
   D CORRECT. The recording says, 'So your old car has broken down again ...'
   E INCORRECT. If you had a car before, or have just passed your test, you already know how to drive.
   F INCORRECT. This is not mentioned.
   Note: with this type of question, if you choose fewer answers than you are asked for, even if they are correct you will <u>not</u> get <u>any</u> marks.

   3 A INCORRECT. The place where cars are sold is called a *showroom*.
   B INCORRECT. Dealers are usually about £800–£1,000 more expensive.
   C CORRECT. If something goes wrong with the car after you've bought it, you can take it back.
   D INCORRECT. This isn't mentioned.

Completing a summary p. 11

1 1 This must be an adjective such as *good/better/safe(r)/cheap(er)*, etc.
   2 This must be a noun: what kind of things can you look through?
   3 The article tells us that this must be a noun.
   4 The answer to this is probably a person or a time.
   5 This must be a noun: what will you not have at an auction?

2 **Note**: there is often more than one acceptable answer to these questions, because the question doesn't state that you have to use words from the text.
   1 *cheaper/less expensive* 'If you're looking for a cheaper car ...'
   2 *(local) papers/adverts* '... by looking in the adverts in your local paper.'
   3 *(obvious) problem/disadvantage/difficulty* 'The obvious problem is that once you've bought the car it's yours and you can't really take it back.'
   4 *by a mechanic/before you buy* '... get a mechanic to check it over for you before you buy it.'
   5 *time* '... you won't really have time to check the car over.'

Skills practice p. 12

1 C
2 B
3 B and E (you MUST have both of these)
4 travel insurance
5 (quite) expensive
6 get home / back
7 too much sun / the (midday) sun
8 clean your teeth / have *or* use ice
9 liquids / fluids / soft drinks / bottled water

Listening for specific speakers p. 13

1 There are three speakers. They greet each other by name.
2 Robert, Anand and Claire.
3 Robert and Claire speak twice. Anand speaks three times.

Listening for specific information/short answers p. 13

1 Qu 2 What is the <u>word limit</u> for the assignment? This must be a number. Qu 3 <u>Where</u> did Robert get his idea for a topic from? This must be a location or a situation: where might you get an idea?

2 1 A *water pollution*
      B *global warming*
   'Oh, you know, <u>water pollution</u> like the oil tanker that broke up and killed all the sea life for miles near Spain, or the kind of thing that's always talked about, like <u>global warming</u>.'
   2 *2, 000 words*
   Robert: What's the <u>word limit</u>, again? Is it 1,500 words, as usual?
   Anand: No, this one's 500 words longer.
   Claire: <u>2,000</u>? Help! We've got more work that I thought!
   3 *an Internet search/the Internet*. 'Have you got any <u>ideas for a topic</u>?' 'I looked through books in the library and some journals, but what worked in the end was <u>an Internet search</u>.'

Completing a table p. 13

1 Questions 1 and 4 ask you to identify the types of pollution. Question 2 must be a date.

2

Pollution problem	Solution provided by	Date completed
(1) *Sewage*	City Council	(2) *1970s*
Boat traffic	(3) *State government*	next year
(4) *Rubbish*	(5) *(Local) divers/ diving clubs*	ongoing project

Classifying p. 14

1

Sea creatures	Stormy weather	Sewage	Emissions
crab	*rain and wind*	*waste water*	*jetski/motor boat fuel*
marine life	*blown*		

3 1 **R** 'I think that they leave the rubbish if any marine life has started living in it – they wouldn't want to make a crab homeless!

2 **S** 'When the weather is bad, especially if there's a lot of rain and a wind blowing towards the shore, the sewage can still be blown in to the beaches.'

3 **B** 'Emissions are actually getting worse …'

4 **S** '… actually, they get much more bothered when they have to swim in waste water, after a storm …'

Spelling p. 14

1 and 2

1 *site* (NOT *sight*). Take care with words that have more than one meaning and spelling, but which sound the same.

2 *6th February.* The month MUST begin with a capital letter.

3 *Wednesday.* Days of the week MUST begin with a capital letter.

4 *suggest*

5 *inexpensive.* Take care with prefixes.

6 *Unemployment*

7 *advise* (NOT *advice*). Note that the sound is different, and here a verb is needed.

8 *politician* (NOT *polititian*). Take care with -*ion* endings.

9 *companies.* Take care with the plural, especially irregular plurals or those which take -*ies.*

10 *successful.* Remember *full* has double *l*, but the suffix only has one *l*.

11 *independent.* Take care with -*ent/-ant* endings.

12 *Receiving.* Take care with the order of *i* and *e*.

3 *constant, perceived* and *sufficient* were spelt wrongly.

Skills practice p. 15

	'A' Levels	Foundation Course
Length of course	2 years	1 year
Number of subjects studied	2–3	(1) *1*
English language support given	often none	(2) *6 hours per week*
Main type of assessment	exam(s)	(3) *continual assessment or assignments and presentations*
Most popular with	(4) *British students*	overseas students

5 academic
6 essay structure/essays
7 global markets
8 It sounds hard/difficult

9 M
10 A
11 M
12 P

Labelling a diagram with numbered parts p. 16

1 1 *Diagram 1:* shows a process. It's a good idea to think about where the process starts and what the most important parts of the process are.

Diagram 2: shows an object. Parts of an object will usually be described in relation to each other, so think about which parts are next to, above or below each other.

Diagram 3: shows a map. For plans, think about which way the plan is orientated, and where features like doors, staircases, etc. are. For maps, look for roads, buildings, rivers, etc.

2 Diagram 1

A *light rays.* '… light rays from the object, … come through the lens …'

B *virtual image.* '… sees a virtual image, which is closer and smaller than the real object.'

Diagram 2

A *face.* '… on the front of the clock, we call this the *clock face* …'

B *pendulum.* '… and behind that, the *pendulum.* That's P-E-N-D-U-L-U-M.'

C *weight.* '… driven by a weight, which is situated in front of the pendulum …'

Diagram 3

A *cafeteria.* '… and the cafeteria is right behind it. You can get to the cafeteria through the Students' Union, or through a separate entrance at the back.'

B *(a large) lawn.* 'If you walk out of the main entrance to the Union, there is a large lawn area …'

C *library.* '… to your left is the library …'

3 Diagram shows a hydroelectric plant. A is behind the dam; B is under the ground; C is under the dam; D joins the plant and leads away from it.

4 A *reservoir.* '… a large artificial lake, called a reservoir. That's R-E-S-E-R-V-O-I-R.'

B *turbine.* 'The turbine is situated underground. Sorry, what was that? Turbine, T-U-R-B-I-N-E.'

C *control gate.* '… under the dam there is a control gate and this can be opened to let the water in.'

D *power lines.* '… by the power lines, shown leading away from the power station.'

Labelling a flow chart p. 17

1 and 2

1 100,000 v
2 power distribution
3 (normal) domestic (electric)
4 (electrical) accidents/accidents with electricity

Sentence completion p. 17

1 1 You need adjectives to complete these gaps. What kind of positive adjectives could be used about hydroelectricity?

2 You need a noun here. What kind of factors limit hydroelectricity?

2 1 *clean/green, little pollution caused* or *sustainable* '… it is a very clean and green method … and it's sustainable …'

2 *(a large) river/reliable water (flow)* '… obviously a large river is needed with a reliable flow of water …'

Listening for signpost words p. 17

1 A. This phrase is used after the speaker has recapped on previously given information, before the speaker moves on to add further, related information.

2 B. In this context, the speaker is drawing attention to a visual, but this could also be used to emphasize a point.

3 C. If this phrase is used, the information that follows is usually related to what went before, but not usually contrasting it.

Skills practice p. 18

1 600 million
2 sediment/sand and mud
3 heat
4 sandstone/limestone (NOT reservoir rock)
5 oil
6 faulting
7 cap rock
8 (access) roads
9 water
10 reserve pit
11 (the) main hole
12 brought in

Key for Reading module

Quiz p. 19

1 B
2 C
3 B
4 A, B, C, E (advertisements can be found in the General Training Reading module)
5 False (unlike the Listening module).

6 True (both the texts and tasks increase in difficulty as the test progresses).
7 False (there are a variety of question types, including multiple choice, short answer questions, completing sentences/notes/charts/diagrams, matching, classifying, etc.).
8 True (although all the topics are of general interest and require no specialist knowledge of the subject matter).

Skimming for gist p. 19

i *What is skin cancer?* This is not correct because while paragraph H does describe some symptoms of skin cancer, the text as a whole does not aim to explain what it is.

ii *Fun in the sun.* This is not correct because the text is about being safe in the sun rather than having fun.

iii *How to treat skin cancer.* This is not correct because treatment for skin cancer is only mentioned briefly at the end of the text.

iv *How to protect yourself from skin cancer.* This is correct because not only does the first paragraph tell you 'it is possible to enjoy the sun and still stay safe', but every paragraph contains information about this.

Matching headings to paragraphs p. 21

iii How the various types of radiation differ

B Sunshine contains three <u>different</u> bands of ultraviolet <u>radiation</u>: UVA, UVB and UVC. Although <u>UVC is the most dangerous</u>, because it is a shorter-wavelength radiation than UVA and UVB, it is screened out by the Earth's ozone layer. <u>UVA</u> used to be thought <u>less dangerous than UVB</u>, but it is now known that <u>both bands can cause skin cancer</u>. It is UVB which causes sunburn. However, <u>both UVA and UVB</u> can age the skin prematurely.

ix A short break in the sun won't hurt, will it?

C Levels of UV rays can vary. A <u>two-week holiday in the Mediterranean</u> will expose you to the same amount of sun as you would get in a year in Britain. <u>Short periods of intense exposure to the sun are thought to be more risky than regular daily exposure</u>, particularly if you have fairer skin. However, even if you have darker skin tones you will burn eventually. You can find out the daily UV rate by watching the solar UV index which has recently been introduced on national weather forecasts across Europe.

viii Is UV exposure through sunbeds as harmful as natural sunlight?

D People haven't really been using sunbeds long enough to be sure of their full effects, but <u>studies indicate that there may well be a potential risk of skin cancer</u>. Because <u>sunbeds</u> use only UVA, you won't get sunburnt. However, this enables you to expose yourself to huge amounts of UVA, something you would not do <u>at the beach</u> where the prospect of getting sunburnt would limit your <u>exposure</u>. Sunbeds will also certainly contribute to your skin ageing more quickly.

iv Sunscreens: the higher the SPF the better?

E The ideal sunscreen to use is an <u>SPF15</u>. This means a sunscreen which gives you fifteen times more protection that you would have normally. An SPF15 sunscreen will absorb proportionally equal amounts of UVA and UVB, and will give you good protection if you are sensible about your exposure. <u>Sunscreens higher than SPF15 tend to lose their balanced effect</u>: the chemicals in an SPF30, for example, will not block UVA rays as effectively as UVB.

The <u>other danger with high SPFs</u> is that people will stay in the sun longer because they think they are better protected. <u>Higher SPFs do not give proportionately greater protection.</u> An SPF15 gives 93 per cent protection, for example, while an SPF34 gives 97 per cent protection.

x How to maximize the SPF of sunscreens

F   It is vital to <u>apply enough sunscreen</u>. In order to receive the protection offered by <u>an SPF15 sunscreen</u>, you would need to put on a 120 ml bottle every day you spent at the beach. Most people do not use nearly that amount, which will <u>reduce</u> the SPF considerably. Moreover, the effectiveness is likely to <u>diminish</u> further when you perspire or wipe your skin with a towel. You should <u>reapply sun cream at least every hour</u> and after swimming, even if you are using a waterproof brand.

vi Other ways to protect yourself

G   Only UVA rays can pass through glass, so <u>you won't get sunburnt</u> <u>sitting by a window,</u> while you can still enjoy the warmth of the sun. Be careful when sitting in the shade, however. You can still get burnt because you will be exposed to rays bouncing off reflective surfaces nearby. This is particularly the case near water. <u>Not all clothing offers</u> <u>effective protection</u>, either. If you can see the light through a piece of clothing when you hold it up, it will not offer much of <u>a barrier to UV rays.</u>

vii What are the first signs of skin cancer?

H   You should keep an eye out for any <u>moles or dark spots on the skin that change in size, shape or colour, become bigger, itchy or inflamed, or bleed</u>. All these <u>may be symptoms of skin cancer</u> and should be checked by a doctor. Once a mole has been identified as a potential melanoma, it is removed under local anaesthetic and sent for examination. Most turn out to be harmless. Of the three forms of skin cancer the two most common varieties – basal cell and squamous cell carcinomas – are easily treatable and rarely fatal, and even melanomas can be treated effectively if caught in time.

The following choices were not correct:

   i *Who is most likely to develop skin cancer?* Paragraphs A and H mention skin cancer, but neither tells you who is most likely to develop it.
   ii *Summer sports and skin protection* This topic is not mentioned in the text.
   v *What is ultraviolet radiation?* Paragraph B describes the differences and similarities between the UVA, UVB and UVC rays, but it does not explain what ultraviolet radiation is.

Pictures, charts and diagrams p. 21

1 Look for clues in words like *both* and *only*.

Use your knowledge of the structure of the text. You know that paragraph D is about sunbeds and paragraph G is about rays passing through glass so save time by looking there for your answers.

	UVA	UVB	UVA and UVB
Can lead to skin cancer			X
Causes sunburn		X	
Can lead to premature ageing of the skin			X
Can pass through glass	X		
Sunbeds use it	X		

2 Check that you understand what the diagram shows. Then find the relevant section in the passage (in this case, paragraph B).

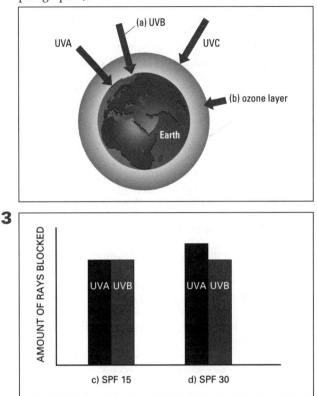

3

Multiple choice p. 22

1 <u>Exposure to the sun</u> <u>on holiday</u> is <u>dangerous</u> because
   A INCORRECT because while the statement is true, it is not specifically about exposure to the sun <u>on holiday</u>.
   B CORRECT. 'Short periods of intense exposure to the sun are thought to be more risky than regular daily exposure.' (para. C)
   C INCORRECT, even though it is true, because it is not specifically about exposure to the sun on holiday.
   D INCORRECT because this is not mentioned in the text.
2 <u>Sunbeds</u> may be <u>harmful</u> because
   A INCORRECT because this is not why sunbeds may be harmful.
   B CORRECT. '… this enables you to expose yourself to huge amounts of UVA.' (para. D)
   C INCORRECT because it is not true.
   D INCORRECT because it is not true.
3 <u>Moles</u>, or <u>dark spots on the skin</u>
   A INCORRECT. The text says, '… keep an eye out for any moles or dark spots on the skin … these may be symptoms of skin cancer …' (para. H)
   B INCORRECT because the text only says *most* are harmless.
   C CORRECT (para. H)
   D INCORRECT. The text does not mention this.

4 Using a <u>high factor</u> (above SPF15) <u>sunscreen</u> can be <u>dangerous</u> because
   A INCORRECT because this statement is not about high factor sunscreens.
   B CORRECT. '… the chemicals in an SPF30, for example, will not block UVA rays as effectively as UVB.' (para. E)
   C CORRECT. 'The other danger with high SPFs is that people will stay in the sun longer because they think they are better protected.' (para. E)
   D INCORRECT because although the text mentions chemicals, it does not say that there are more in a high factor sunscreen.
   E INCORRECT because although this statement is both true and mentioned in the text, it is not relevant to the question.
5 In order for an <u>SPF 15</u> sunscreen to <u>actually offer you</u> 15 times normal protection, you <u>need to</u>
   A INCORRECT. This is true, but not relevant to the question.
   B CORRECT. 'It is vital to apply enough sunscreen.' (para. F)
   C CORRECT. 'You should reapply sun cream … after swimming …' (para. F)
   D INCORRECT. This is not mentioned in the text.
   E INCORRECT. This is not mentioned in the text.
   F CORRECT. '… the effectiveness is likely to diminish further when you perspire or wipe your skin with a towel.' (para. F)
   G INCORRECT. This is not relevant to the question (and would not offer you extra protection).

Guessing meaning from context p. 22

1 1 *sufferers* is a noun
   2 *40 per cent of sufferers from melanoma will die.* This tells you that sufferers must be alive – in fact they are people who have an illness.

2 *apply*: use, reapply, put on; *protection*: sunscreen, effectiveness; *reduce*: diminish

Skills practice p. 23

1 ii Zoo life in Europe shortens elephant lives
2 vii
3 iv
4 v
5 12
6 up to 65 years
7 up to 10
8 30
9 Reason 1: A
10 Reason 2: B
11 Reason 3: D
12 90% = European zoo elephants without grazing
13 48% = World zoo elephants held in Europe
14 66% = European female zoo elephants separated very early from their mothers
15 B
16 A
17 C

Skimming for gist p. 26

Answer: B What is the best way to prevent bushfires burning out of control?

Scanning to find information quickly p. 26

1 Paragraph **A**, iv: 'Tens of thousands of hectares of national park may be disappearing in smoke …', '… the contentious issue of what is causing the bushfires, and how they can be stopped.'

Paragraph **B**, ii: '… a growing body of scientists who say the only way to limit the blazes is to set the bush on fire during the winter months.' 'Australian species such as the eucalyptus and banksia often require the passage of bushfires to allow their seeds to germinate …'

Paragraph **C**, i: 'But John Connor … disagrees that burnoffs on national park land are the answer.' 'A lot of native plants can survive maybe three fires in 20 years, but more often than that and you'll end up with nothing but eucalyptus in the forest.'

Paragraph **D**, iii: 'Environmentalists believe the real concern around the fires should be the indication they give of the coming impact of global warming …' '… many scientists … say that there hasn't even been an increase.' '… you hear a lot more about the fires because there's more people living cheek-by-jowl with the fire areas.'

Paragraph **E**, v: '… people are moving into these dangerous areas and are not taking any of the precautions which they should be taking …' 'People need to put space between their houses and the forest, keep away from the higher areas and clear out dry undergrowth from their gardens, otherwise it will only encourage the fires …'

2
1 Para. B. This paragraph is about the scientists' point of view. It is also one of two paragraphs in which Phil Cheney's name is mentioned.
2 Para. D. This paragraph is about people living near the bush.
3 Para. E. This paragraph is about safety when building houses and gardens near the bush.

Short answer questions p. 28

1 'There's this misunderstanding of <u>the nature of fire</u>," said <u>Phil Cheney</u>, of the Commonwealth <u>Scientific</u> and Industrial Research Organisation (CSIRO). "Most people still don't accept that <u>it's</u> a **natural ecological phenomenon** …'
2 'The three areas worst affected by the fires that hit Sydney before Christmas were all on the <u>bush fringes</u> and had seen a massive <u>influx</u> of **city-dwellers** in recent years, <u>keen to escape the inner city and enjoy the pleasures of the bush.</u>'
3 'Many dwellers <u>on the bush fringe</u> choose to make the most of their new location by planting gardens using flammable native plants, rather than the more retardant imported species, and <u>building homes</u> on the **tops of ridges** to enjoy the views of bushland. <u>These last are a particular fire risk,</u> …'

Extract	Paraphrase
1 The bushfires came to Melbourne today in a more gentle manner than usual. **No** firestorms raging close to suburban streets and **houses reduced to ash** ...	**Different:** **No** houses were destroyed by bushfires in Melbourne on the day the article was written.
2 **More and more people are living in the bushland** ... **a massive influx of city-dwellers.**	**Same:** There has been a **large increase** in the number of **people from the cities** moving into the bush.
3 'Of course you **need some sort of burning close to houses** ...' (says John Connor)	**Same:** John Connor agrees that **limited burning just near people's property** is necessary.
4 **Environmentalists are pitted against a growing body of scientists** who say the only way to limit the blazes is to set the bush on fire during the winter months.	**Different:** **Many** but **not all** scientists **disagree** with environmentalists about the best way to limit the blazes.

Understanding paraphrasing p. 29

A paraphrase may look similar in meaning, but be careful to look out for words like *all, every, no*, etc. These can change the meaning.

True, False or *Not Given* and *Yes, No* or *Not Given* p. 29

1 NOT GIVEN. Some Australian *plant* species need bushfires to survive. You can tell that eucalyptus and banksia are plants, not animals, from other clues in the text, '... allow their seeds to germinate.' (para. B) 'A lot of native plants ... nothing but eucalyptus...' (para. C) The text says nothing about Australian animals.

2 YES. 'Many dwellers on the bush fringe choose to make the most of their new location by ... building homes on the tops of ridges to enjoy the views of bushland.' (para. E)

3 NO. 'A lot of native plants can survive maybe three fires in 20 years ...' (para. C)

4 NO. '... so far there is little reliable information to indicate whether fires have in fact been getting worse.' (para. D)

5 YES. 'Environmentalists believe the real concern around the fires should be the indication they give of the coming impact of global warming ...' (para. D)

6 NOT GIVEN. This may be true, but it is not mentioned in the text.

Recognizing opinion p. 29

1 1 F. '... he remembers flying 600km (373miles) ... and seeing only two breaks in the continuous fire front.' (para. E)

2 O. 'John Connor ... disagrees that burnoffs on national park land are the answer.' (para. C)

3 F. 'The urban areas of Sydney and Melbourne have doubled since 1960.' (para. D)

4 O. Phil Cheney says there has been 'no measurable change in the incidence of fires since the 1960s.' (para. E) but he does not give any evidence to support his statement.

5 O. 'Environmentalists believe the real concern around the fires should be the indication they give of the coming impact of global warming.' (para. D)

2 1 JG. Para D: '... you hear a lot more about the fires because there's more people living cheek by jowl with the fire areas.'

2 MB. Para E: 'People need to put space between their houses and the forest ... otherwise it will only encourage the fires.'

3 JC. Para C: 'Bushfires may be natural, ... but the sort of forest management needed to prevent risk to property is definitely not.'

4 PC. Para B: 'Most people still don't accept that it's a natural ecological phenomenon, and until we do that we're not going to be able to prevent these out-of-control fires.'

5 PC. Para E: 'The provision of an implicit guarantee of protection from the emergency services ... they should be taking.'

3 Statement 3 is correct because the writer does not at any point give his own opinion but presents the opinions of others combined with some facts.

Skills practice p. 30

1 F
2 B
3 H
4 D
5 processed (foods)
6 90%
7 2 grammes
8 strokes, heart attacks
9 TRUE
10 FALSE
11 NOT GIVEN
12 TRUE
13 CSM
14 CO
15 SO
16 FC
17 CSM
18 B

Skimming for gist p. 33

C is the best answer as it covers most of the main ideas in the text.

Summary completion p. 33

1 1 Noun (the use of the article *the* tells us this)
2 Noun (followed by a verb)
3 Noun (something you can *take*)
4 Adjective (*was more* ... tells us this is part of a comparative structure)

2 1 *speed* 'An Israeli researcher says drivers who listen to fast music in their cars ...' 'Warren Brodsky at Ben-Gurion University in Beer-Sheva, wondered if tempo had any effect on driver behaviour.' (lines 4–14)

2 *Students* 'To find out, he put a group of 28 students through their paces on a driving simulator. Each student drove ...' (lines 14–17)

3 *risks* 'As the tempo increased, Brodsky found drivers ran (took) more risks ...' (lines 28–29)

4 *distracting* 'He also monitored the drivers' heart rate and found <u>that it fluctuated less when they were listening to music of any kind compared with no music at all.</u> This lack of variation, he suggests, shows that <u>music is distracting the drivers</u> and making them less alert.' (lines 40–45)

Guessing meaning from context p. 34

1 and 2

1 *virtual.* '... <u>on a driving simulator.</u> Each student drove round the *virtual* streets of Chicago ...' (lines 15–17)
2 *laid-back.* '... a variety of styles, ranging <u>from</u> *laid-back* George Benson ballads <u>to the ultra-fast</u> numbers beloved of clubbers.' (lines 21–23) *Laid-back* is used in contrast to *ultra-fast*.
3 *concedes.* 'Brodsky <u>concedes</u> that behaviour on a simulator may not translate into the same behaviour on the road. "<u>But I think</u> it's got to be taken seriously," he says.' (lines 36–39)
4 *monitored.* 'He also *monitored* the drivers' <u>heart rate</u> ...' (line 40)
5 *fluctuated.* '... and found that it *fluctuated* less when they were listening to music of any kind compared with no music at all. <u>This lack of variation</u> ...' (lines 40–43) *Lack of variation* is another way of saying *fluctuated less*.
6 *attitude.* 'The study has changed Brodsky's own *attitude* to in-car music ... "<u>I'm now more careful in my choice of music.</u>"' (lines 50–56)

Note completion p. 34

1 *alert* '... shows that music is distracting the drivers and making them less alert.' (lines 44–45)
2 *slower* '... choose slower pieces of music ...' (lines 47–48)
3 *distracted* '... turn down the volume so they are less distracted.' (lines 48–49)

Understanding paraphrasing and sentence completion p. 34

1 1 has a hand in their fate (lines 3–4)
2 the research is worrying (line 9)
3 put ... through their paces (lines 14–15)
4 relatively loudly (line 26)
5 to maximise its effect (lines 26–27)

2 1 F 'But it is <u>not only the speed</u> at which people drive <u>that is the problem</u>: <u>the speed of the music</u> they are listening to <u>also</u> has a hand in their fate.' (lines 1–4)
2 G 'The tempo ranged <u>from a slow</u> 60 beats per minute <u>up to a fast and furious 120 beats per minute or more.</u>' (lines 23–25)
3 I '... drivers who listen to fast music in their cars may <u>have more than twice as many accidents</u> ...' (lines 4–6)

3 1 *slower tracks.* '... may have more than twice as many accidents as those listening to <u>slower tracks.</u>' (lines 5–7)
2 *for seven years.* 'The students had an average of <u>seven years</u>' driving experience.' (lines 19–20)
3 *played relatively loudly.* 'All the music was <u>played relatively loudly</u> to maximise its effect.' (lines 26–27)
4 *medium-paced.* '... drivers had more than twice as many accidents when they were listening to fast tempos as when they listened to slow or <u>medium-paced</u> numbers.' (lines 33–35)

1 an alternative
2 diesel
3 safer
4 cultivate
5 deserts
6 quantities / amounts
7 investment
8 specifically
9 F
10 A
11 D
12 C
13 A
14 E
15 vegetable oil / sunflower oil / soybean oil / opium poppy oil
16 carbon monoxide / carbon dioxide / soot / sulphur (oxides)

Key for Writing Module

Quiz p. 37

1 B
2

	How long should you spend on this task?	Minimum number of words
Task 1	20 minutes	150
Task 2	40 minutes	250

Task 2 carries more marks than Task 1 so don't spend more than 20 minutes on Task 1.

3 B But don't forget that occasionally the question may require you to describe a process.
4 A
5 A
6 C

Understanding data p. 37

1 1 Figure 3
2 Figure 1
3 Figure 4
4 Figure 2

2 1 F
2 E
3 D
4 C
5 A (North America or Asia / Oceania 25%)
6 B (Western Europe 38%)

3 1 Figure 2
2 Figure 4
3 Figure 3
4 Figure 1

4 Figure 1   1   eating in restaurants and cafés
           2   expenditure in pounds (£) per week on eating out or takeaway meals
Figure 2   1   Western Europe
           2   11 million tonnes
Figure 3   1   1994–2002
           2   newspapers
Figure 4   1   different continents
           2   the total world population in different years

Language focus: Expressing figures and quantities p. 38

1 1 £7, £2
2 1998, 8.5
3 4%, 30%
4 7, 317

2 1 *more than trebled* (from 203 million to 726 million) means it *increased (more than) three times*. Similar expressions include *more than doubled* which means *twice* or *quadrupled* which means *four times*.
2 *twice as many* (from 6 to 13 million) means *two times as many*. Similar expressions include *three or four times as many*, etc.
3 *exactly the same* (about 24%). A similar expression is *identical*.
4 *Very little* (less than 5%). Use *little* for uncountable nouns, *few* for countable nouns.
5 *a quarter* (25%). Similar expressions include *a half, three quarters, a third* but do not use complicated fractions, eg *three fifths*. Percentages are also an option.
6 *slightly more* (7% compared to 5%). A similar expression is *slightly less*. These phrases are more appropriate than *a little more/less*.
7 *Half as much* (£2 compared to £4). Use *much* for uncountable nouns (*money* in this case), *many* for countable nouns.
8 *much more* (£10 spent per week compared to £4 per week). A similar expression is *much less. Far more/less* can be used with adjectives, eg *far more expensive* as an alternative to *much more expensive/much cheaper*.

The opening statement p. 39

1 A This simply uses the same words as the heading for the chart. Remember copying will not gain you any marks.
B The chart does not provide information about ages so it has not been described correctly.
C This sentence provides an accurate description of the general trends shown in the chart and is therefore the best opening statement.
D The data has not been interpreted correctly (the number of first marriages did not rise) so the statement is not appropriate.

2 1 A This is a simple but truthful analysis of the data.
B This comment is also true but the analysis is not adequate.
2 A Although this information is true, it is not appropriate as an opening statement as it is too specific.
B This statement shows the general trend over this period.

3 *Suggested answer*:
In general car sales increased significantly from 1970 to 1990 and from the beginning to the end of the century the number of car owners in the UK rose dramatically.

Language focus: Describing change over a period of time p. 40

1 A – increased sharply
B – fell gradually
C – remained stable
D – fluctuated

2 increased sharply – rose dramatically
fluctuated – varied
fell gradually – decreased steadily
remained stable – stayed the same

3 *shows* – present simple for general truths
rose, doubled – past simple for completed actions in the past
were sold – past simple passive used to focus on the action rather than the person who performed the action

4 1 *similar* – this means the pattern is nearly, but not exactly, the same
2 *doubled* – a more appropriate, economical word
3 *remained stable* – a more academic phrase to describe a constant pattern
4 *highest* – this is a collocation
5 *figures* – an appropriate academic word when describing numbers
6 *slight* – the most appropriate way of describing a little / small change

5 1 increased
2 rose steadily
3 sharp fall
4 increased dramatically
5 remained stable
6 rise

6 0 A *steady increase/gradual rise* in sales. Sales *increased steadily/rose gradually*.
1 A *slight drop/slight fall* in sales. Sales *dropped slightly/fell slightly*.
2 A *sharp increase/sharp rise* in sales. Sales *increased sharply/rose sharply*.
3 *reached a peak*
4 *remained stable*
5 *fluctuated*
6 A *sharp drop/sharp fall* in sales. Sales *dropped sharply/fell sharply*.
7 A *steady decrease/gradual fall* in sales. Sales *decreased steadily/fell gradually*.

Skills practice p. 42

Suggested answers:
1 Since 1961, the percentage of people in Great Britain owning one or more cars has increased significantly.
2 In 1961, about 70% of the population did not have a car but in 2000 this figure had fallen to about 30%.
3 Since the late sixties, the number of British people owning only one car has remained stable at about 45% of the population.
4 From 1961 to 2000, the percentage of the population who have two or more cars has increased steadily, from about 2% to nearly 30%.

Selecting and grouping information p. 43

1 A and E are important as they reveal the most significant information (the most popular sports for young men and women). Sentence D is the next most relevant sentence to include (as the difference between most and second most popular sport is quite slight). Sentences B, C and F are not particularly important sentences in terms of key information.

2 Sentences B, D and E show the best ways of grouping key information as they compare and contrast the most popular sports. Although sentences A and C group information, A is too general while C is specific yet cannot really be considered as key information. Sentence F does not really group information in a logical way.

3 A This answer describes the data in a repetitive and therefore, boring style. It does not attempt to select the key information or group information clearly. This type of answer is therefore not satisfactory.

B This answer is well-organized, focuses on important information and groups key features in a logical way. Specific references to figures are provided and the language is of an appropriate academic style. It is therefore the best answer.

C Here the language is weak in terms of grammar and vocabulary: omission of articles and relative pronouns, unnecessary *to* before activity, plural forms wrong (*woman*), word formation wrong (*approximate*), inappropriate linkers used (*and* at start of sentence) and style is very repetitive (*young men/women*).

Language focus: Expressing comparison and contrast p. 44

There were 7 examples of the language of comparison and contrast in this sample answer.
1 playing football was the most popular sporting activity
2 whereas young women prefer swimming
3 cycling and swimming are popular with both sexes
4 cycling is far more popular than swimming
5 while slightly more young women swim than cycle
6 young men prefer football to any other sport
7 it was the least popular sporting activity

Skills practice p. 44

1 1 It shows how many people travelled by air from the UK to different destinations in 1991 and 2001.
2 It represents the destination countries.
3 It represents the number of people travelling.
4 They show the number of people travelling in 1991 and 2001.
5 The number of people travelling to most destinations has more or less doubled in ten years.

2 Important information. Writer has misinterpreted the chart by saying passengers are <u>coming from</u> different countries when they are all from the UK <u>going</u> to different countries. However, the main point is included – that the figures have increased.

Length. Approx 135 words - too short

Style. Generally OK but inappropriate use of contractions (*it's*), lack of variety of linking words, eg replace '*also*' with '*in addition*', countries not capitalized.

3 Here is the corrected *sample answer.*

From the bar chart it is easy to see the increase of international passenger movements by air in 1991 and 2001. Ten countries were researched and we can see that passenger movements by air were much higher in 2001 than 1991.

Spanish passengers travelled most in 1991, followed by those from the USA and then France. By 2001, in some cases the increase had more than doubled, for example Spain and the Irish Republic. In some countries there was only a slight increase such as Switzerland and Portugal.

The data also shows that international air passenger movements from Spain and America were much higher than other countries in 1991 and 2001. In the ten year period the figures increased significantly.

Model answer

The chart compares air travel by passengers from the UK to a number of other countries in 1991 and 2001. In all cases there was an increase in passenger movements.

By far the most passengers went to Spain with over 27 million people travelling in 2001. This figure had more than doubled since 1991. The second greatest volume of traffic was with the US, with 17 million air passenger movements, an increase of approximately 8 million in ten years. Other countries that showed significant rises were the Irish Republic with nearly 10 million passenger movements and Italy and the Netherlands with about 7 million people travelling to each of these places.

At the lower end of the scale roughly 4 million people travelled to Switzerland and Portugal in 2001 but these figures had also increased since 1991.

The chart confirms the increased popularity of air travel for UK passengers in the period 1991 – 2001.   (154 words)

Comments:
There is a clear opening statement which has paraphrased the words describing the bar chart. The most significant features are highlighted ('By far the most…') and specific details are given (27 million). Other key information is described clearly and accurately and the report finishes with an appropriate sentence to sum up the main points.

Describing a process p. 45

1 *First stage*: The student contacts the institution …
Final stage: The student has now enrolled …

2 and 3
1 The student <u>contacts</u> the institution about the English course. (*present simple active*)
2 The student <u>goes</u> to the institution and <u>completes</u> a placement test. (*present simple active/ present simple active*)
3 The student <u>is interviewed</u> by an experienced teacher. (*present simple passive*)
4 The student <u>is placed</u> in a class at the appropriate level. (*present simple passive*)
5 The necessary forms <u>are completed</u>. (*present simple passive*)
6 The student's details <u>are put</u> on the computer. (*present simple active*)
7 The student <u>pays</u> the fees for the course. (*present simple passive*)
8 The student <u>has now enrolled</u> and <u>is given</u> a student card. (*present perfect active/ present simple passive*)

4 A does not clearly specify what the activity is
B *improving your English* is not really a procedure – progress in English should happen after the course starts
C correct

5 *Suggested answers*:
1 *next put* a teabag into a cup
2 *after that pour* the boiling water into the cup
3 *after a few minutes take out* the teabag
4 *then add* some milk and sugar and stir
5 *finally drink* the tea

6 *Sample answer*:
The procedure for enrolling for an English course at a language school or college is as follows:

First of all, the student contacts the institution by phone or post about the English course. Then he or she goes to the school or college and completes a placement test. After that the person is interviewed by an experienced teacher and is placed in a class at the appropriate level, for example beginner or advanced. At the next stage, the necessary forms are completed and then the student's details are put on the computer. Finally, he or she is told to pay the fees for the course. This completes the procedure and the student has now enrolled at that particular school or college. They are given a student card and are ready to start lessons.

Note: one or two details have been added (methods of contacting the college and different levels). If you add details, they must be relevant and based on fact.

Skills practice p. 46

1 a – 10
b – 5
c – 6
d – 9
e – 2

2 *Model answer:*

In order to make better quality paper from waste paper, the following process takes place:

First of all the paper is collected. After this it is very important that paper clips, plastic and staples are removed. The waste paper is then sorted into specific categories such as newspapers, computer paper and magazines. Next, the ink must be removed. This is done by soaking the paper and then breaking it up in large washers and adding chemicals. Depending on the end paper product, and other materials are added such as bleach or dyes as well as other chemicals.

The materials are then passed through a heavy roller which squeezes out all the water before the pulp is pressed and flattened into thin sheets. After that these sheets are dried in furnaces and the final paper product is polished and treated before cutting into sheets or rolls. Finally the product is packaged for distribution.   (151 words)

Understanding the instructions and the question p. 47

1 A False. It is recommended, **not** compulsory.
B True. Topics are of general interest and will not be on specific subjects.
C False. Expressing views is one of the most important aspects of this task.
D True. Providing supporting evidence and information is also vital.
E False. Writing should include some personal views but aim to be academic and impersonal in style.

2 A Discuss.
B What are your opinions on this?
C To what extent do you agree with this statement?

Understanding the topic and the task p. 47

1 A The question doesn't ask about visiting other countries but talks about living overseas.
B The question does not mention studying specifically.
C Correct.

2 A Correct.
B The question does not ask for a list of positive points about living overseas (although one or two could be mentioned).
C The question does not ask the candidate to compare living in the UK with other countries.

Skills practice p. 47

1 1 Main topic: high crime rates in cities
Task: suggest best ways to reduce high crime rate
2 Main topic: increased world tourism
Task: comparison of advantages and disadvantages of mass, global tourism
3 Main topic: animal testing
Task: give your opinion on whether animal testing is ever acceptable and if so, when and why

2 • to consider how things are different and how they are similar: *compare*
• to show a good reason for something: *justify*
• to compare two things to show how they are different: *contrast*
• to question whether something is true or accurate: *challenge (ideas)*

3 1 i – suggesting a solution to the problem of crime in cities
2 iii – comparing and contrasting the positive and negative effects of global tourism
3 ii – evaluating this view of animal testing and giving your opinions on this issue

Brainstorming and planning p. 48

1

Problems of living overseas	Ways to make living overseas easier
language	learn the language
culture and lifestyle	join a club or society
accommodation	find out about the place before you go
food and drink	sample local food
miss friends / family	keep in contact with friends / family
people	try and meet / speak to local people
religion	observe / respect local customs

4 C This is the most appropriate essay structure.

5 A This is the best structure because it mentions the main difficulties of living overseas in the introduction. It then describes how some problems are unavoidable in the second paragraph. It then discusses ways to make the experience easier in paragraph 3 before summing up in the final paragraph.
B This is quite well structured but the contents of paragraph 2 are not relevant to the task.
C This lacks overall structure (no conclusion) and is also irrelevant to the task.

THE INTRODUCTION P. 49
1 This opening almost repeats the question word-for-word.
2 Although giving opinions is a valid response, this introduction is too personal. The task does not require the positive points so this information is irrelevant.

Exclamation marks are not appropriate in IELTS writing tasks.

3 This opening briefly mentions why people live overseas. It states that although this can be positive, certain problems are likely to occur and then gives some examples. This introduction is a balanced response to the question – the content is relevant to the task and it is written in an appropriate style.

THE MAIN BODY P. 50

1 1 Topic sentence = F
   2 Supporting evidence = A, C, D, E
   3 Link with next paragraph = B

2 *Model answer:*
There is no doubt that living overseas can be very difficult at times. Adjusting to a new culture can often take weeks or months. During this period it is not uncommon for people to feel very homesick and really miss their friends and family. Not being able to speak the language very well can make life even more difficult. In addition, other problems may arise from different lifestyles, types of food or accommodation. However, there are a number of ways to reduce the difficulties.

All paragraphs should follow this basic pattern:

Topic sentence ⟶ Main idea

Supporting ⟶ Supporting
sentences   evidence

Concluding or ⟶ Sum up main
bridging sentence   idea / link to next paragraph

3 Sequencers: *firstly, secondly, finally, (thirdly, after that)* etc.
Reason or result: *as a result, because/as, therefore, so, (consequently)* etc.
Contrast: *however, although, despite this (whereas)*, etc.
Extra information: *in addition, besides, moreover, (what is more, furthermore)* etc.

4 1 *Firstly* – the first suggestion
   2 *In addition* – extra information about the first suggestion (could be *secondly*)
   3 *Secondly* – the second suggestion
   4 *therefore* – a reason for the second suggestion (could be *so*)
   5 *so* – a reason for the third suggestion
   6 *However* – showing a contrast to third suggestion
   7 *Finally* – a fourth and final suggestion

5 1 find out information about the other country and speak to people who have lived abroad
   2 learn the language
   3 try to make friends with local people and keep in contact with people from your own country
   4 be open-minded

6 1 Many women have successful careers nowadays. *However*, compared to men, not many women have senior positions.
   2 In England I live with a host family. *Therefore/As a result/Consequently*, my spoken English has improved rapidly.
   3 Many students go overseas to study *because/as* they believe the quality of education is higher.

CONCLUSION P. 51

1 A This conclusion shows the writer's opinion in one sentence. It is clearly too brief, too general, and does not review earlier contents of the essay.
   B This conclusion sums up the main idea of this task and refers back to the suggestions made earlier. The final sentence clearly illustrates the writer's view on the points discussed earlier. It is the best conclusion.
   C This conclusion sums up by listing three suggestions covered in the essay and states that following these would be appropriate. The tone is too personal and listing is not really suitable in this short essay format.

2 *Model answer:*
In conclusion, settling into life in a new country can cause many problems. Some difficulties cannot be avoided, for example those related to language or culture. However, there are a number of solutions such as studying the language or making friends with local people. Living abroad can often be a very positive experience and you should try to enjoy it as much as possible.

Skills practice p. 52

1 Topic: crime in cities
Task: suggest solutions to this problem

2 *Suggested answers*

Other problems in cities	Crimes	Ways to prevent/reduce
congestion	*murder*	*more police*
overcrowding	*burglary*	*stricter punishments*
pollution	*mugging*	*individual protection*

3 Paragraph 1 – introduction – there are other problems, but crime is the biggest
Paragraph 2 – method 1 – increase police
Paragraph 3 – method 2 – stricter laws/punishments
Paragraph 4 – method 3 – better security
Paragraph 5 – conclusion – sum up ideas

4 A Too general
   B Appropriate
   C Not strictly true

5–8 See *Model answer* below

Model answer:
There is no doubt that numerous problems exist in most modern cities. Although traffic congestion, pollution and overcrowding often occur, many people believe that crime is the most serious problem in urban areas. Indeed, television and newspaper reports often tell us that crime continues to rise. However, it is possible to tackle this serious issue in a number of ways.

One approach would be to increase the number of police. If more police were on the streets, whether on foot or in patrol cars, criminals would be less likely to commit crimes and people would feel much safer. Having more police visible at night would be particularly beneficial.

A second possibility would be to make laws stricter and punishments more severe. This could involve increasing fines or lengthening prison sentences. If a criminal has to pay more money for doing something illegal or would face more time in prison then I believe this is likely to reduce the crime rate.

Thirdly, methods to increase security might deter potential criminals. For example, more effective alarms in houses and cars. This would reduce burglary and theft. In addition, more information about home security would also be useful. In terms of personal safety, rape alarms or even small weapons could prevent some attacks on people.

In conclusion, although crime is a major problem in most cities in the world, the situation can be addressed by adopting the methods mentioned above. In this way, the negative effects could be reduced and people living in cities would feel much safer.

Further practice p. 53

Model answer:
Before any new product is put on the market, whether it is a cosmetic product, or a potentially life saving medicine, the producers will want to make sure that it is safe for humans to use. A common way of doing this is to test the product on animals.

Many people feel that this is unacceptable because it assumes that an animal life is somehow less valuable than a human life. Opponents of animal testing point out that the animals involved often suffer great pain and fear, and argue that we have no right to do this to them for our own benefit.

On the other hand, it cannot be denied that animal testing has helped scientists to make great discoveries in the field of medicine, providing effective drugs against cancer, heart disease and other potentially fatal illnesses. Supporters of animal testing argue that many lives have been saved this way.

I would agree that there may be some benefits to using animals to test new medicines, although I would prefer such testing to be kept to a minimum. Increasingly, there are new ways of testing products, using cell cultures, which need not involve animals at all. However, even when this is not possible, I cannot agree that it is necessary to test cosmetic products on animals. There are already thousands of cosmetic products on the market, with no need for further development and testing. Exploiting animals in this way is, in my opinion, completely unacceptable.

In conclusion, I would not agree that testing products on animals is never acceptable, but it should be reserved for essential scientific work.   (269 words)

Comments:
The essay has been clearly structured into five paragraphs: an introduction giving reasons for this situation, arguments against, arguments for, writer's opinion (strong opposition) and a clear, concise conclusion. The essay contains a wide range of grammatical structures and uses a variety of linking words to give cohesion (*on the other hand, however,* etc.). There are also numerous ways in which opinions are expressed (*Many people feel …, I would agree …, in my opinion …*). Overall, the topic has been addressed thoughtfully and appropriately.

Key for Speaking module

Quiz p. 54
1 B

2 1 True
      2 False. This is not an IELTS task.
      3 True
      4 True
      5 False. You have to speak for 1–2 minutes.
      6 False. You are given a card with a topic and some prompts to help you.
      7 True
      8 True
      9 False. This is the most challenging part of the module as you are asked to talk about more abstract issues and ideas.

Talking about familiar topics p. 54

Possible questions:

Your studies
How long have you been studying English?
Why is it important for you to learn English?
Who was your favourite teacher at school? Why did you like their lessons?
What are you planning to study?
Why are you taking IELTS ?

Your previous work experience (if any), your current job or your future career plans
What do you do? (Be careful with this question. It means *What is your job?*)
What are / were the best things about your job?
What are your ambitions?

Your family/home life
Tell me about your family.
What does your father do? (or mother)
Do you live with your family?
Do you have a large family?
How long have you been here?
Tell me about where you are living at the moment.

Your country
How would you describe your home country / home town?
What are the best things about life in your country?
How is life in your country different from life here?

Your hobbies and interests
What are your main hobbies?
Do you enjoy travelling?
What do you usually do at the weekend?
Are you interested in playing sport?
What type of music / films do you enjoy most?

Giving a good answer p. 54

2 A Not enough information. A good example would be: *Mr Wallis, our chemistry teacher. He made the subject really interesting, and although he was very strict, he was also quite funny.*

B Doesn't answer the question. Be careful of learning phrases by heart and then just using them even when they're not appropriate. A good example would be: *I started learning English at school when I was only 10, but the lessons weren't very good. I've been studying properly for about three years, though.*

C A good answer. This answers the question and adds a little extra information as well. It also sounds fluent and is accurate.

D A good answer. Again, this answers the question and gives a little extra information. The beginning, *Oh definitely …* sounds very natural.

E Not enough information. Don't make the mistake of thinking that the less you say, the fewer mistakes you will make! The examiner needs to be able to assess your fluency and you are expected to give more than one-word answers. A good example would be: *No, I don't. I live with three other students in a shared house. It's quite close to college, so it's convenient.*

F Doesn't answer the question. Be careful with *How long + present perfect*. Remember this refers to past time up to now. A good example would be: *I came in April, so I suppose I've been here about six months now.*

G Not fluent enough. It's good to show you have a wide vocabulary, but it's more important to communicate fluently. A good example would be: *It's a small house near to the town centre. It's not very attractive, but it's comfortable and the rent's quite cheap.*

H A good answer. This answers the question, gives some extra information and is correct and fluent.

Identifying strengths and weaknesses p. 55

Although the student's answers are not monosyllabic, many of the responses are rather brief and could be more fully developed (*Five years. I studied at high school in China*). There are a few grammatical inaccuracies (*I usually do play ping pong, the product major is charcoal*) and a rather limited range of vocabulary but some evidence of wider lexical knowledge (*managing director, fitness clubs*). Some inappropriate use of vocabulary (*charcoal town*). Pronunciation is generally good, but the intonation is heavily influenced by her native language and would benefit from flowing more freely. There aren't many words or phrases to make her responses sound more natural or to gain more time and there are quite a few hesitations.

Overall, the student would need to focus on improving fluency and producing more extended responses as well as aiming to show a wider, more accurate use of language.

Planning your answer p. 56

1 and **2**
Describe <u>an occasion</u> when <u>you</u> have been <u>successful</u>.
You need to talk about one occasion or event in your life (any time up to the present) when you were successful.
- where and when you were successful – give the background (school, home, college, work, how old you were)
- how you were successful – *say what happened (won a race/passed an exam)*

- what you had to do – *give examples: studied hard/worked hard/prepared in some way/asked for help*
- how you felt – *very happy because/very excited because …*

Giving extra information p. 56

Talk about <u>an important day</u> in <u>your life.</u>
- when this day was – *the day my football team got promoted*
- if you were alone or with others – *with my brother and others in crowd*
- where you were / what happened – *got to football ground, waited for game to start, lots of people, final goals – we won!*
- and explain why this day was important to you – *first time team had ever been promoted*

Sample answer:
OK, the important day in my life that I'm going to talk about happened about four years ago. This was the day my football team got promoted. The team, er, had played well all that season and had reached the finals, and my brother and I were, er, were both keen supporters and we both followed the team, er, for about fifteen years. It was a very exciting day for, for the team because they'd never been promoted to, er, out of the division into a higher division in their history.

My brother and I got to the football ground about lunchtime and waited for the game to start as the crowd built up- there were about 10,000 people there that day. The game swung from side to side, with, first of all, our team scoring and then the opposing team scoring twice, which was why it was fantastic when our team scored two goals in the last five minutes to win the day and gain promotion to the higher division. The noise at the final whistle was amazing and we were all incredibly excited. I don't think I've ever been to a game where there was such a great atmosphere, before or since. We really celebrated that night, but the next morning, I could hardly speak from all of the shouting I'd been doing!

The speaker has included the key points, then added extra details to make the talk more interesting.

Identifying strengths and weaknesses p. 57

Student 1
This answer is quite short and does not satisfactorily cover all the points on the card. However, it has quite a good range of language and is quite accurate.

Student 2
Level of communicative ability is high. Some hesitations but clear that the speaker has a very natural style and produces a measured, thoughtful response to the points on the card.

Follow-up questions p. 57

1 1D   2E   3C   4F   5B   6A

Expanding answers p. 57

1 *Possible answers*
Yes, I think it's a good idea – especially as you get older <u>because</u> it can help to keep your body active. It's important to make time for exercise, even when you're busy, <u>so</u> I try to go to the gym three times a week. If I'm honest, <u>however,</u> it's usually more like twice a week.

2   Well, no, I don't think there is really. It probably just seems
    that way because it's reported in all the newspapers <u>and</u> on
    the television. I think there has always been quite a lot of
    crime in big cities, <u>although</u> there may be more crime <u>such
    as</u> house-breaking in rural communities these days.
3   Well, it's certainly useful to have one. <u>On the other hand</u> I
    find it really annoying when I'm on the train and
    everyone's talking into their mobile phones. I think there
    should be more control about when and where people can
    use them.

Linking ideas p. 58

1 1 because
    2 so
    3 and
    4 however, on the other hand
    5 such as

Model answers:
1   Do you think smoking will be banned in all public
    places?
    *I hope it will! I hate going into smoky pubs and restaurants.
    However, I don't think it's very likely to happen here for a
    while even though it's already happened in some countries.*
2   Do you prefer to go out or stay at home in the evening?
    *I prefer going out. It's so boring just staying at home and
    watching TV. However, I can't always afford to go out when I
    want to.*
3   Do you think that email has made our lives easier?
    *It's amazing being able to keep in touch with my friends and
    family so easily, but I can't help thinking that email has
    actually created more work for most people. I often get 40–50
    messages a day – far more than I ever got on paper or by
    phone.*
4   Which is better: living in the countryside or in the city?
    *Well, on the one hand, it's certainly cleaner and quieter in the
    countryside, but I think I would miss the nightlife if I lived
    there – it could be a bit too quiet! I might move to the
    countryside when I'm a bit older.*
5   Are qualifications important?
    *Yes, definitely. I strongly believe that you must have good
    qualifications these days if you want to get a good job. Maybe
    it was different in the past, but nowadays employers expect
    more.*
6   How likely is it that computers will be able to do your
    job in the future?
    *I doubt very much if computers could take over the job of a
    nurse. OK, they could do some of the monitoring of patients,
    but they'd never be able to give the support we do.*
7   Would you rather watch sport or play it?
    *Well, it probably depends on the sport. I'd rather watch
    boxing than actually do it. It's not as dangerous! But I like
    playing and watching football. I particularly like going to see
    live matches.*
8   What do you think the consequences of global warming
    will be?
    *It's bound to have more and more of an effect on the weather. I
    think there's a good chance that the climate of Britain will
    change quite noticeably over the next few years, which could
    cause all sorts of problems.*

Key for Practice test

Listening
1   C
2   B
3   Moseley
4   third (floor)
5   No
6   £520
7   B
8   375 Greenfield Rd/Road (NOT Green Field)
9   357629
10 4.15
11 two or three/2–3
12 up the coast/north
13 the sun
14 hat/cap
15 well-known/obvious
16 (to) towards the shore (beach)/against the rip
17 across the current/parallel to shore
18 lessens/reduces/gets weaker
19 swim alone
20 a lifeguard
21 Biology
22 cotton
23 expense/they're expensive/cost
24 eat harmful bugs (insects)/pollinate crops
25/26/27 A, C and D in any order
28 painted/applied
29 flowers
30 wings
31 partnership
32 (a) person/human being
33 one person
34 every year/yearly/once a year
35 make (the) (important) decisions
36 capital/money/investment
37 shares (of stock)
38 employees/workers
39 profit/money
40 B

Reading
1   C
2   S
3   C
4   S
5   E
6   N
7   N
8   Y
9   NG
10 Y
11 D
12 B
13 A
14 A
15 F
16 C
17 primary role
18 the (country's) economy
19 unacceptable
20 7
21 environmentally sustainable

22 cereals
23 (making) paper
24 water (supply)
25 B
26 F
27 C
28 G
29 D
30 F
31 A
32 C
33 over 20 years
34 negative/aggressive
35 wound healing
36 ten years later
37 measuring
38 heal
39 conflict
40 physical

Writing

Model answer for Task 1:
In general cinema attendance increased significantly from 1984 to 2000. However, the number of people watching films at the cinema varies with age.

Since 1984, cinema attendance has risen considerably across all age groups, but the increase was greatest for the 15–24 age group, which rose from about 18% in 1984 to over 50% in 2000. Though the figures fluctuated between 1990 and 1995 this age group still went to the cinema more than any other group.

There was also a substantial rise in cinema attendance among older people (35 plus). In this case the figures increased over this period from about 2% to over 10%.

Cinema attendance of 7 to 14 and 25 to 35-year-olds followed a similar pattern from 1984 to about 1997, which was characterized by a gradual increase until about 1994 followed by a decline after this date. However, from 1999 the trends differed in that 7 to 14-year-olds went to the cinema less frequently while cinema attendance of 25 to 35-year-olds was on the increase. (172 words)

Model answer for Task 2:
More and more women are taking on the roles of housewife and mother at the same time as doing a full-time job. However, it is not always possible to have a fulfilling and successful career and still give total commitment to home and family.

Many women are forced to go back to work after their child is born for financial reasons. For some, a career is more important than full-time motherhood. Whatever the reason, it is true to say that there are more working mothers these days. Indeed many employers now recognize the valuable contribution that women make in the workforce and have introduced measures such as on-site childcare facilities and flexible working hours to accommodate their needs. Many women who want to advance up the career ladder may feel it is better to postpone having a family until later on in life and some choose not to have children at all.

It can be very difficult to cope with the demands of a full-time job and also have the responsibility of raising a family. Many working mothers find it increasingly difficult to devote quality time to their families. For this reason some women do not return to work after having children while others choose to work part-time. For many this is a preferable option as it enables them to follow a career yet also gives them more time to bring up and look after their children.

In conclusion, although recent changes in the workplace have made it easier for working mothers, most women find it extremely difficult to give full commitment to both work and family and it is often the case that compromises have to be made to make it successful.
(280 words)

Recording scripts

Listening module

Recording 01

[K = Keiko, S = Stephan]

K: Um, excuse me. Do you know where the accommodation office is?

S: Yes, of course. Are you a new student?

K: Yeah. I only arrived here yesterday, so I still feel a bit lost.

S: I've only been here a couple of weeks, but it doesn't take long to find your way around. The campus isn't that big. The accommodation office is in the main building.

K: Is that the three storey building by the lake?

S: No – look, it's that big building there behind the trees. The one with the glass front. Go in through the main door – then up the steps.

K: You mean the door on the right-hand side?

S: Yeah. Then, when you get inside, go straight down the corridor, to the far end, and turn left. You'll see three doors on your left – accommodation is the middle one.

K: So, I go along the corridor, turn left, and it's the second door on the left?

S: That's right!

K: Thanks very much for your help.

S: No problem, see you around. My name is Stephan, by the way.

K: Oh, OK, great. I'm Keiko.

Recording 02

[K = Keiko, AO = Accommodation Officer]

K: Excuse me, am I in the right place to look for accommodation?

AO: Are you a student here?

K: Yes, I just arrived yesterday, and I was looking for some help with finding a place to live.

AO: Well, you've come to the right place! What sort of accommodation are you looking for?

K: I'm not sure really. Could you tell me what's available?

AO: Of course. There are three kinds of accommodation that we deal with – home stays, college halls of residence, or private lets.

K: Home stays? Is that where you live with a family?

AO: Yes, that's right. Usually you have your own room, and maybe your own bathroom, but you live with a local family and they provide you with meals, access to a washing machine, all of that kind of thing. That's $130 per week, or $90 without meals.

K: Yes, I did think about doing that. It would be a good way to practise my English, but I think I'd really prefer to live with people more my own age, other students, for example.

AO: Of course. Well, the college has a small residential block, with rooms for 50 students, but it's very popular and I think at the moment it's full.

K: That's a shame.

AO: Yes, students like it. You have your own study bedroom, with a bed, a table, chair and a washbasin, and then you share a bathroom and kitchen with four other students.

K: It sounds nice. Never mind. What was the other option that you mentioned?

AO: The other one is, um, private lets. These are flats and houses owned by private landlords, not the college, but we make sure that you are paying a reasonable price so it's a bit easier than just looking in the newspaper to find a flat.

K: That sounds good. Would it be for one person or more?

AO: It depends. Mostly, flats are for three or four students, but there are sometimes one bedroom flats available.

Recording 03

[K = Keiko, AO = Accommodation Officer]

K: So, how can I find out about the flats or rooms that are available at the moment?

AO: Well, I can give you all that, but if you wouldn't mind, first of all, I'll take down a few contact details and then if something suitable comes up, I'll be able to tell you.

K: OK, great.

AO: So, what's your name, please?

K: Keiko Jenkins.

AO: Sorry, could you spell that for me, please?

K: Of course. It's K-E-I-K-O and my surname is J-E-N-K-I-N-S.

AO: Thank you. What's your nationality? I thought that you must be Japanese, but Jenkins is an English name.

K: Yes, it is. My father is English, and I have British nationality, but I grew up in Japan, so I feel more Japanese.

AO: How interesting. So, Keiko, where are you staying at the moment?

K: At the Sunrise Guest House. It's number 562 Green Park Road.

AO: 562 Green Park Road. Fine. And do you have a contact number?

K: I've got a mobile. It's 07785 265 981.

AO: Sorry, I didn't quite get that. Was it 256 891?

K: No, 07785 265 981.

AO: Thanks. And email? Have you got an address you can access easily?

K: Yeah, it's keiko@hotmail.com

AO: That's fine. OK …

Recording 04

15
50
162
£3.25
47%
0.54
12,651

Recording 05

U Y J O G X I P Z W H A Q R E B

Recording 06

1 forward slash
2 hyphen
3 colon
4 semi-colon
5 dot

Recording 07

1 A: Sorry. What was that name again – Sir Anthony …?
   B: Sir Anthony Winton, that's A-N-T-H-O-N-Y.   W-I-N-T-O-N.
2 A: So what's the answer, then?
   B: 34.92.
3 A: Could I just take your address?
   B: Certainly, it's 15 Sparrow Lane. Sparrow is S-P-A double-R-O-W.
4 A: How high is Everest?
   B: Let me look it up. Mm, it says here 29,030 feet.
5 A: What's his name again?
   B: Michael MacWilliams – M-I-C-H-A-E-L . M-A-C-W-I double-L-I-A-M-S.
6 A: … and I live at 286 Banbury Road.
   B: How do you spell Banbury?
   A: B-A-N-B-U-R-Y.
   B: Thanks.
7 A: So, what did I get in the test?
   B: 74%.
   A: Great!
8 A: Who's your favourite author?
   B: Mm, that's hard, but I think it must be Janet Gates.
9 A: So what was the number again?
   B: 0121 674 95 double 4.
10 A: Do you have a reference number on that letter?
   B: Um, yes, I think so. Here it is … reference number 654/120084.
11 A: OK, is it Mrs J Smith?
   B: No. Mrs J Robson-Smith.
12 A: … and what's your address there?
   B: Flat 3, 547 Oxford Road.
13 A: What was the web address of that company?
   B: I think it was www. bht.co.uk
14 A: Could I make an appointment, please?
   B: Which doctor do you usually see?
   A: Dr. Brown.
15 A: What's the registration of the car?
   B: N 770 CES.

Recording 08

[D = Dan, RM = Restaurant Manager]

RM: Hello, Giovanni's Italian Restaurant. Can I help you?
 D: Hello, yes, I hope so. I'm phoning to enquire about booking a party at your restaurant. Do you cater for large groups?
RM: Yes, we do, but the maximum we can seat together is 24.
 D: Oh, that's fine. I think there'll be about 18 of us.
RM: Fine, no problem. We have a large room at the back of the restaurant that we usually use for groups. It means that you are not disturbed by the other customers.
 D: That sounds fantastic. Does it cost extra for that?

RM: No, no, no, we just ask that you spend at least £10 per person on your meal.
 D: That seems reasonable. Is it one long table?
RM: No, it's three round tables. Each table will seat eight people. We find that's a bit more of a friendly way of eating – you can talk to more people, and there's more space on the table for the food!
 D: Oh, yes – that's important!
RM: So when do you want to come?
 D: Well, we'd like a Friday or Saturday night really, maybe April the 15th?
RM: Let me see. Oh, I'm sorry, the 15th is already fully booked. I have a space on the 16th – that's the Saturday. Is that any good?
 D: It's not really what we wanted, but it'll be OK.
RM: Or the week before? I have a space on Friday the 8th.
 D: That's a bit early, really. No, the 16th will be fine.
RM: Usually when we have larger groups we do a set menu – three courses and coffee for a fixed price. Is that what you were looking for?
 D: Is there any choice about the different courses?
RM: But of course! We don't expect everyone to want exactly the same thing! For each course there is a choice of three different dishes, it may be a prawn cocktail to start with for example, or a soup, or maybe a plate of Italian ham and cold meat – we call it *antipasto*.
 D: Great. Just one other thing … I know that a few people in the group are vegetarian. Do you do a vegetarian option?
RM: Absolutely. At least one of the choices for each course is made without meat or fish.
 D: That all sounds great. Is coffee included in the price, did you say?
RM: Certainly … cappuccino, espresso whatever you like.
 D: OK. So how much do you usually charge for the set menu?
RM: For parties of under ten people, it's £15 a head. If you have more than ten it's a bit cheaper!
 D: As I said, I think it'll be about 18 people.
RM: In that case, we can do it for £12 a head. That doesn't include wine or drinks, of course.
 D: No, I understand. Well, that all sounds very good.
RM: There's only one other thing – for larger groups like this, we like to take a deposit a week before you are planning to come – 10% would be fine.
 D: Oh, OK. 10% – that'd be 10% of £12 multiplied by 18 people … how much is that?
RM: Wait, I have a calculator here … um … it's £21.60. Call it £25 to make it a round number.
 D: OK, so I need to give you £25 a week before the 16th of April?
RM: Perfect!
 D: Right, well, I'll finalize the numbers and get back to you in the next couple of weeks to give you the deposit.
RM: Lovely. We look forward to your visit, Mr …
 D: Glover, Dan Glover.
RM: Sorry, can you spell that, Mr Glover?
 D: Sure, it's G-L-O-V-E-R.
RM: Thank you. And could I take a contact telephone number for you?
 D: Of course. My work number is probably best – it's 01452 863092.
RM: Thank you very much. We look forward to seeing you.
 D: Goodbye.

Recording 09

Hello again, and welcome to *You can do it,* the programme that aims to help give you inside information into life's trickier tasks. Today we're going to talk about the different ways there are of buying a used car, something that very few people feel very confident about. And let's face it, a mistake can be expensive, as well as very inconvenient.

So your old car has broken down again, and you're feeling that this really is the end for it and it's not worth repairing, or maybe you've just passed your test and are desperate to get out on the road. You look at new cars, but they are so expensive – what can you do? Well, there are three main places to look for a used car, and they all have their advantages and their disadvantages. The first place, and probably the one that most people would go to first, is a used car dealer. These are showrooms where you can go and choose from a range of second-hand cars. Obviously some places are bigger than others, and some are better than others. On the whole, this kind of place is probably the safest way of buying a car as you'll get some kind of warranty. Typically this is about three to six months, maybe a year on a newer car, so if something goes wrong with the car after you've bought it you can take it back – you've got some kind of guarantee. The problem, of course, is that you'll pay for it. Cars from dealers are usually about 800 to £1,000 more expensive than the same type of car bought privately. Quite often dealers will offer you a discount, especially if you've got an old car to trade in, and that might make it seem very attractive. Many will offer you credit, too, so that you don't have to pay for the car straightaway, but it's always good to remember that although this is an expensive way to buy a car, it's probably the safest.

Recording 10

If you're looking for a cheaper car, one way to go about it is to buy a car privately – usually by looking in the adverts in your local paper. This can be a really good way of buying a car, but takes quite a bit more effort. You have to get the paper each week, look through all of the adverts to see if there is anything suitable, make phone calls to arrange a time to see the car, and then travel to view it. The obvious problem is that once you've bought the car it's yours and you can't really take it back. It's probably a really good idea, if you know nothing about cars, to get a mechanic to check it over for you before you buy it.

The final place that you can buy cars is at auction. There are auction rooms up and down the country where cars are sold to whoever will pay the highest price for them. This is definitely the cheapest way of buying a car, but it's also the most risky because you won't really have time to check the car over. So unless you're a mechanic, or don't mind taking a risk, this probably isn't the best way of buying a car. You can find some real bargains, though!

Well, we're now going over to our reporters who have been trying out these different methods, let's hear what they think …

Recording 11

Good morning, everyone. It's good of you all to come, especially those of you who have come straight from sports coaching. For those of you who don't know me, my name is Jenny Arnold and I'm the university Health and Fitness Officer. Today we've got another in our occasional health lectures. This time, with the summer drawing closer and many of you off on holiday, I wanted to talk a bit about being safe and keeping healthy while you're travelling.

Actually, the time to start thinking about this is a few weeks before you go away. If you're going to a foreign country, it's a really good idea to check out any vaccinations that you need. Your GP can tell you this, or you can call up NHS Direct, the free medical telephone service and talk to one of the nurses there. Don't leave it until the last minute, because for some of the vaccinations you'll have to have two shots with a week or two between them. Your local doctor, as well as giving you advice, can give you most of these injections and they should be free as you are students, but you may have to pay for things like malaria tablets if you are going to a country where malaria is a problem.

The other thing that you should arrange before you leave is travel insurance. You might think that this is a waste of money, and it can be quite expensive if you are going somewhere exotic, or doing dangerous sports or activities such as diving or skiing. But it does mean that you can relax and enjoy your holiday, knowing that if anything terrible did happen to you, then you'd be covered financially, at least, and could get home safely.

While you are away, especially if you are going somewhere hot, as many of you probably want to then do take care in the sun. Most of us, here in the UK, don't see much sunshine for most of the year, and if you suddenly expose your skin to the midday sun, without any sun cream, you'll just end up looking very red and feeling very sore. It's not a good start to your holiday and there can be dangerous long-term consequences from skin cancer, too.

Finally, take a few sensible precautions about eating and drinking to avoid illness. Be careful about drinking the water if you are visiting less developed countries and remember that this includes things like cleaning your teeth and ice in your drinks. It's always fun to try new food when you are away, but you might find that you have a slightly upset stomach for the first couple of days, just while you get used to it. Make sure that you keep drinking plenty of liquid – bottled water is best, but soft drinks and fruit juice are OK in moderation too. Take a couple of tablets for it if it gets very bad. You can get these from any chemist here.

Well, I hope that that's been helpful. If you have any other questions, I'm in room 5B, just pop in and ask me.

Recording 12

[R = Robert, A = Anand, C = Claire]

R: Hi there, Anand. What are you up to?

A: Hi Robert. Hi Claire. I'm just having a look at the group project that we've got to do this term.

C: The ecology one?

A: Mm, that's the one.

R: Well, we've probably caught you at a good time then. Claire and I were hoping we could have a bit of a chat about it with you. We're doing it together, aren't we? Have you got a minute now, or are you busy?

A: No, it's OK. Now is a good time. We do need to think about starting work on it, don't we?

C: The main question seems to be knowing where to start. I know that we have to identify an environmental problem somewhere in the world and look at what kind of measures have been taken to limit it, but it's difficult to narrow it down to one!

Recording 13

[R = Robert, A = Anand, C = Claire]

A: Yeah, trying to think of a topic is a problem, isn't it? I've been thinking about it, but it was only the major disasters that I could think of – you know the recent ones that have been in the news.

R: Like what?

A: Oh, you know, water pollution like the oil tanker that broke up and killed all the sea life for miles near Spain, or the kind of thing that's always talked about, like global warming.

C: Do you think we should choose something like that?

A: No! Oh, it'd be such a major piece of work if we did.

R: What's the word limit again? Is it 1,500 words, as usual?

A: No, this one's 500 words longer.

C: 2,000? Help! We've got more work than I thought!

A: Have you got any ideas for a topic?

R: One or two. I was having trouble, too, I looked through books in the library and some journals, but what worked in the end was an Internet search.

A: What did you search for?

R: I put in *environmental* and *disaster* and then did some other searches using words like *sea,* or *river* or *soil erosion.*

A: And that helped?

R: Well, sort of! It gave me a lot of information. My first search came up with 372,000 sites! Obviously I didn't look through them all, but browsing through some gave me an idea for the assignment. How about looking at the problems of pollution in Sydney Harbour?

Recording 14

[R = Robert, A = Anand, C = Claire]

C: The harbour? It'd be local, but it looks pretty clean to me!

R: It is now, but it used to be a real problem. Sewage, for example, used to be emptied directly into the harbour.

A: Yuck! Imagine swimming in all of that waste water. It's not a nice thought, is it?

C: You said it *used to be* a problem …

R: Yes. Sewage is taken out in pipes a long way out to sea now. The City Council constructed them in the 1970s. Unless there is very bad weather, it's solved the problem.

C: What other problems are there?

R: Well, of course there is a fair bit of pollution from the traffic on the harbour.

C: You mean all of the boats?

R: Yes. There are the ferries, of course, but also the commercial and trading vessels. It's still an issue. The State government has set targets for reduction in emissions by next year, but they can't stop boats using the harbour, can they?

A: I guess one of the other problems must just be people dumping rubbish – bottles, plastic bags, stuff that people can't be bothered to dispose of properly.

R: Yeah, that's right. There's quite a good story behind that one, though. It's an ongoing project – it's not finished yet, but a lot of it has been removed.

C: How did they manage that? It must be a really difficult job.

R: Local diving clubs who like to dive in the Harbour go down and pick up old bottles and things like that off the bottom of the sea. I think they have a special day once a year to do it.

Recording 15

[R = Robert, A = Anand, C = Claire]

A: So, do you think those are the three main areas we should look at for our assignment?

R: Well, that seems to make sense to me, at least it's reasonably limited.

C: I think we should make some notes, so that we can divide up the work.

A: Yeah, that's a good idea. So, tell us again, what do the divers do?

R: It's in their interests, really – they want to dive in clean water, so they go down and pick up old bottles and cans, things like that. I think that they leave the rubbish if any marine life has started living in it – they wouldn't want to make a crab homeless!

C: That's great, isn't it?

A: So the Harbour is really clean, now?

R: Well, not bad. When the weather is bad, especially if there's a lot of rain and a wind blowing towards the shore, the sewage can still be blown in to the beaches.

C: Not very nice … but I suppose it's not very often. I heard that people using jet skis and small motor boats was a problem.

R: Yeah, I read about that, too. Emissions are actually getting worse, despite what the government wants to happen.

C: You would think that that kind of thing would make people who live here really angry.

R: You would, but actually, they get much more bothered when they have to swim in waste water, after a storm …

Recording 16

1 The college is on the site of an old castle.
2 The meeting will be held on the sixth of February.
3 Please hand your essays in by next Wednesday.
4 We suggest that you take the test in May.
5 The course is inexpensive and highly beneficial.
6 Unemployment rose dramatically in 2001.
7 I would advise you to do your homework.
8 He was a very successful politician.
9 Different companies have different management systems.
10 He had a very successful career.

11 Studying abroad can help you become more independent.
12 Receiving unwanted emails, or *spam*, is a growing problem.

Recording 17

[B = Brenda, C = Cathy]

B: Hi Cathy, I haven't seen you around for ages. Where have you been?

C: Oh, I've been here, but I've been studying really hard, and not going out much, so that's probably why I haven't seen you. I seem to spend all of my time in the library, or in my room with my nose in a book!

B: So your course is hard work?

C: Yes, it is, but it's mainly because we're coming to the end of the year and I've got a few major assignments to get in.

B: Actually, I wanted to talk to you about your course. You're on the Foundation Programme, aren't you?

C: Yeah, that's right. Are you thinking of doing it next year?

B: Maybe. I want to study at a British university, but I'm not sure whether it would be better to do 'A' levels, or a Foundation Course. Which do you think would be better?

C: Well, the big advantage of a Foundation Course is that it only takes a year – 'A' levels take two.

B: Really? That's a big difference!

C: Mm, it is. With 'A' levels, you usually study two or three subjects, and you may not get any extra language support. With a Foundation, you study five or six modules, but they are all connected to one subject – usually the one you want to study at university, for example Business, or IT, and you do extra English classes, too – mostly about six hours a week.

B: That sounds helpful.

C: And another good thing about it is that you don't have to take any exams on the Foundation – well, not any major ones, anyway. All the marks come from continuous assessment, you know, from your assignments and presentations, that kind of thing. 'A' levels have some continuous assessment, but a lot of your marks come from the final exam.

B: That's a bit scary … So, if the Foundation is so much shorter and has no exams, why would anyone want to do 'A' levels?

C: Good question. I didn't want to and Foundation Courses tend to be popular with students from overseas, but I think most British students do 'A' levels. It's part of their education system. Also, to be honest, if you get good 'A' levels, it gives you a lot more choice about which university you can go to. All British universities recognize 'A' levels, but some don't recognize Foundation Courses, especially if you want to do one of the more popular courses.

B: So are you saying it's hard to find a place at a university with a Foundation Course?

C: No, there is still a lot of choice, just not as much as with 'A' levels.

B: What's the course like, anyway?

C: Hard work! But I've enjoyed it. The one I'm doing combines Business Studies and English, so I study different business modules for 15 hours a week, and then we study Academic English – that's six hours.

B: And what are the English classes like?

C: They're good – I find them really helpful. They're not like the general English classes I was doing before, though. We do a lot of work on reading academic-type texts and writing in the sort of style that you need to use at university. It's quite hard. Even when I feel that the language I'm using is mainly accurate, the thing that's really different to my language is how essays are structured in English. We're doing quite a bit of IELTS practice, too, at the moment, because most of us are planning to take it next month.

B: So you have to take the IELTS exam?

C: Most universities want you to, yes.

B: What's the other part of the course like?

C: The business modules? They're really interesting. We look at economic theory and marketing strategies, global markets, all kinds of things. I had a bit of an advantage, because I studied Business in high school in France and so I know some of the information already, but it's in a bit more depth than I did before and studying it in English makes a big difference. It can be difficult to understand everything that your lecturer says, sometimes. We have a lot of written work to give in too – assignments, mainly.

B: It sounds very hard.

C: And I've got to give a 20 minute presentation next week using Powerpoint …

B: Really?

C: But despite all that I'm really enjoying it!

B: So have you applied for any universities, yet?

C: Yes, but it's difficult, because the university I really want to go to hasn't given me an offer yet.

B: Which one is that?

C: Ainsley University. I've had a conditional offer from Millford, and they only want IELTS band 5.5, which I'm sure I can get. I've heard that Ainsley usually ask for 6.5, and that's a bit more difficult. Then there's Parmouth, but I haven't heard from them yet, either.

B: Which one is the better university?

C: Overall, Ainsley is, but people say that Millford has a great Business School.

B: What's Millford like as a place to live?

C: Well, it's in Westhampton, actually. I've heard the city is pretty good, but Parmouth is better – it's close to the sea.

Recording 18

Diagram 1

So light rays from the object, which is a small leaf in this illustration, come through the lens to the eye, but because they are diffracted, or bent by the lens, the eye sees a virtual image which is closer and smaller than the real object.

Diagram 2

Pendulum clocks have always been popular. Their technology is quite straightforward, as we can see if we look at this diagram. You can see the hour and minute hands on the front of the clock, we call this the *clock face*, and then if we look behind the face, we see the main gear train, and behind that, the *pendulum*. That's P-E-N-D-U-L-U-M. This is the part of the clock that we hear ticking. This is driven by a weight which is situated in front of the pendulum and by slowly pulling downwards on a string, the weight pulls the gear train around.

Diagram 3

The campus is quite a large one, and most people take a few days to find their way around. The Students' Union is the large, single storey building in the middle of the campus, and the cafeteria is right behind it. You can get to the cafeteria through the Students' Union, or through a separate entrance at the back. If you walk out of the main entrance to the Union, there is a large lawn area that is very popular in the summer, and then, to your left is the library, and over to your right is the Porter Building.

Recording 19

Good morning, everyone. Well, moving on from our discussion last week about oil-fired power stations, I want to move on today to a form of power that many would argue is far superior. It provides 25% of all electricity worldwide and is the only power generator in common use that uses renewable energy – I am, of course, talking about hydroelectric or hydropower plants – energy from water. Hydropower plants are actually based on a rather simple concept – water flowing through a dam turns a turbine, which turns a generator. The idea is nothing more than a water wheel and the principle has been in use for thousands of years.

Some hydropower plants are built using waterfalls, but the majority of them rely on a dam that holds back the water in a river, and creates a large artificial lake, called a reservoir. That's R-E-S-E-R-V-O-I-R. If you look at this diagram, you will see that the main powerhouse is built in front of the dam and that the transformer is inside, seated on the generator. The turbine is situated underground. Sorry, what was that? Turbine, T-U-R-B-I-N-E. Right, as you can see, under the dam there is a control gate, and this can be opened to let the water in. It travels by gravity, through a tunnel, called the *penstock*, to the turbine, and then out of the outflow to the river below the dam. This movement of water turns the turbine, which generates electricity. The amount of power generated can be controlled by the amount of water taken in by the control gate, so that, for example, at night, when less electricity is consumed, the supply can also be reduced. The power is converted by the transformer into very high voltage current, which is then taken to where it's needed by the power lines, shown leading away from the power station.

Recording 20

Let's look at this final process in a little more detail. As we've said, the power leaves the generator and enters what is known as a *transmission substation* at the power plant. This substation uses large transformers to convert the electricity up to extremely high voltages. This may be over a hundred thousand volts. The reason for this is to reduce losses of power when it's transported over very long distances. On average, electricity travels about 500 km from where it's produced to where it's used. That's a long way! The next stage in the process is a local power substation. This has several functions – it 'steps down' the electric voltage, that is, it reduces it to something that can be used domestically, it also distributes the power, and finally, has circuit breakers so that the power can be switched off if necessary. The power coming out of the substation and along wires to houses is still at 7,200 volts, and so, close to each house, is a transformer drum or box, which lowers the voltage to 240 volts – normal domestic electric service. Finally, each house has a fuse box, or a circuit breaker, which are safety devices to ensure that accidents with electricity are minimized in the home.

Recording 21

Let's get back to our hydroelectric plant. One of the main advantages, of course, of generating power in this way, is that it is a very clean and green method. It takes advantage of a naturally occurring process and so there is little pollution caused, and it's sustainable – it will keep going long after coal and oil have run out. However, there are some difficulties. It depends a lot on the geography of the country – obviously a large river is needed with a reliable flow of water and it's often difficult to find a place which is suitable for a dam. Creating a large, artificial lake involves flooding a river valley, and this is not often popular with the people whose homes will be left underwater! Usually people are compensated and resettled – given homes in a new location – but this can cause other social problems.

Recording 22

Good afternoon. Today we start the first in a series of five lectures on the petroleum industry. Today we'll be looking at how oil is formed, and how it's found by oil companies. Over the next few weeks we'll be examining the process of extraction, and of processing, in more depth.

Right, as you know, in the developed world in particular, oil is a vital commodity. In a single month, the demand for crude oil in the USA can be over 400 million barrels. So where does it come from? And how did it get there? Between 10 million and 600 million years ago oil was formed from the remains of tiny plants and animals, mostly invisible to the human eye, called *plankton*. When they died, the plankton sank to the bottom of the sea, into the sand and mud. Because of all of the sand and mud, usually called *sediment*, there was little or no oxygen and so the plankton was broken down to form organic layers. We call this mixture of organic matter and rock, *source rock*. Over millions of years, more and more sediment was deposited, and the weight of these layers put enormous pressure and heat on the source rock. Because of this, the organic matter, which, you will remember was originally from our plankton, was distilled into crude oil, and could flow out of the rock. Some rock, such as sandstone, is very porous, which means that liquid can be absorbed into it, a bit like a sponge. The crude oil collects in rock like sandstone, or perhaps limestone, and it is called *reservoir rock*.

So what we have now is crude oil, inside sandstone, or maybe limestone, under the ground. Now, if you look at the diagram on your handouts, you'll see that this reservoir rock can be trapped in the Earth by various methods. In all three cases, the natural gas and oil is trapped below a layer of hard rock that it can't flow through. This is known as *cap rock*. The first illustration shows *folding*; strong horizontal movements push the rock together into a fold and trap the oil and the natural gas, which sits on top of it. The second drawing shows *faulting*, that's F-A-U-L-T-I-N-G. Here the layers of rock crack, and then, when one side shifts upwards or downwards, the oil is trapped against the fault line. Thirdly, we have *pinching out*. In this case the cap rock comes up from below, and is actually squeezed upwards into the reservoir rock, leaving two pockets of oil.

Finding oil is an expensive business, and although modern technology such as satellite imaging, has made it much easier, the success rate for finding oil fields is still remarkably low. For every ten potential sites found, only one will yield a new oil field. When one has been found, however, there are certain procedures that need to be followed. The first thing is to settle all the legal issues over who owns the land. As drilling is usually in desert areas or the sea, this is not always as straightforward as you might think! After this has been done, the crew start to prepare to drill. Let's look at a land example to give us the idea. Firstly, the land has to be cleared and levelled and access roads may have to be built, depending on what is available. Water is needed for the drilling process, so there must be a source of it locally. If there isn't one, then a well has to be dug. After this, the crew dig a *reserve pit* – basically a big hole lined with plastic to protect the environment. The reserve pit is used to get rid of rock cuttings and drilling mud during the process. Finally, several holes are dug for the rig, and then a large, rectangular pit, called a *cellar* is dug where the actual drilling hole will be. This gives the workers room to move about when they start to dig the main hole. They start doing this with a smaller drill, and then when they have the hole started, the main rig is brought in.

Speaking module

Recording 23

[E = Examiner, S = Student]

E: Why are you taking IELTS?
S: Generally, er, because the universities need it, and, er, need to achieve, er, a high score of English level.
E: How long have you been studying English?
S: Five years. I studied at high school in China.
E: How would you describe your home country or your home town?
S: My home town is, er, charcoal, charcoal town. The product major is charcoal. And um, it's not really nice town, it's industrial town.
E: What are the best things about life in your country?
S: Um, Chinese food ... dumplings, something like that.
E: What do you usually do at the weekend?
S: I usually do, play ping pong and swimming in China, and go to fitness clubs.
E: What do you hope to do in the future?
S: I want to be a managing director.

Recording 24

OK, the important day in my life that I'm going to talk about happened about four years ago. This was the day my football team got promoted. The team, er, had played well all that season and had reached the finals and my brother and I were, er, were both keen supporters and we both followed the team, er, for about fifteen years. It was a very exciting day for, for the team because they'd never been promoted out of the division into a higher division in their history.

My brother and I got into the football ground about lunchtime and waited for the game to start as the crowd built up – there were about 10,000 people there that day. The game swung from side to side, with, first of all, our team scoring and then the other team scoring twice, which was why it was fantastic when our team scored two goals in the last five minutes to win the day and gain promotion to the higher division. The noise at the final whistle was amazing and we were all incredibly excited. I don't think I've ever been to a game where there was such a great atmosphere, before or since. We really celebrated that night, but the next morning, I could hardly speak from all of the shouting I'd been doing!

Recording 25

Student 1

I met my friend in China six years ago. My parents and his parents are, um, workmates and he and me are, were, classmates in high school. And, um, he's in England for three years, and so am I. Er, we study together and live together as well. He studies harder than me and he's, er, very generous and he's, er, quite intelligent as well. So he plays a very important place in my life.

Student 2

OK. I have a friend called Jolie. She's Chinese and we met in the first class, the first English class. We were paired up to do an assignment and that's how we became friends. Umm… I've known her for about five months and it's been fun. We do…we help each other assignments and we go for movies and cook together, have dinners and stuff and just have fun talking, laughing, singing. Um… I think she's played a very important part in my life because she…she…I admire her motivation and dedication and I think she's a very intelligent person and very strong-willed and …something… a lot of her character I wish I had in my life so that's why I think she's played an important role in my life.

Recording 26

1 A: Do you enjoy playing sports?
   B: Yes, definitely. I particularly enjoy outdoor ones.
2 A: Would you like to go there again?
   B: Possibly. It would depend on who I went with!
3 A: Do you think it will be easy to get a job in IT?
   B: I expect so. It's a growing industry.
4 A: Have you ever been to any other countries in Europe?
   B: Yes, a few. France, Spain and the Czech Republic.
5 A: Would you consider doing the same sort of job again?
   B: I don't think so. It wasn't really for me.
6 A: Would you recommend the holiday to other people?
   B: No, not really. It wasn't very good value for money.

Recording 27

[E = Examiner, S = Student]

1 E: Do you think smoking will be banned in all public places?
   S: It's hard to believe that, because, people in China, not like in England, when they drinking and eating, they probably like to give you a cigarette to smoke, and I would like to stop smoking in public buildings and public libraries, because it hurts the people.

2 E: Do you prefer to go out or stay at home in the evening?
   S: I prefer to stay in, because after class I feel very tired.

3 E: Do you think that email has made our lives easier?
   S: Mm, yes, I think so, because email makes distance, um, shortly, makes distances reduced and, um, you can connect your friends where ever he or she is.

4 E: Which is better: living in the countryside or in the city?
   S: I much prefer to live in the countryside. It's quite quiet there, and the fresh air is very, very good.

5 E: Are qualifications important?
   S: For my opinion it's not really important, well, it is important in China, but personal ability is much more important, because in people's eyes, your goals can be anywhere.

6 E: How likely is it that computers will be able to do your job in future?
   S: Um, all jobs to do with calculation and, um, numbers, but I don't think computers can help us to think about things.

7 E: Would you rather watch sport or play it?
   S: I do like to play it. I like to play basketball and swimming. Yes, I do like to watch it as well, but not really, you know, strong as to play it.

8 E: What do you think the consequences of global warming will be?
   S: Mm, actually I don't know much about global warming, but I think it's a really pollution to take very seriously.

Practice test

Section 1

[JT = John Taylor, EA = Estate Agent]

EA: Good morning, William's Estate Agents. Julie speaking. How can I help you?

JT: Oh, hello, um, good morning. I'm new to the area, and I'm looking for a flat or a small house to rent. Do you deal with rental properties?

EA: Oh yes, we have quite a number of properties for rent. What area are you looking for?

JT: Well, I've only recently moved here, so I don't have any definite area in mind, but I'm studying at the university, so I'd like to be within a reasonable distance of that.

EA: Is that Aston University, or Birmingham?

JT: Birmingham.

EA: Oh, OK, and what sort of thing were you looking for?

JT: As I said, a flat or a small house – there's only me, so I don't need a lot of space.

EA: One bedroom, then?

JT: Probably two – I'm doing a Masters degree, and I find it easier to work at home, so I'd like to have an extra room for a study.

EA: Do you want a garden or a garage?

JT: No, not really. A garden would be nice, but it's not essential … oh, and I don't have a car.

EA: And what sort of price were you looking to pay?

JT: I don't really know what price properties go for around here, but I guess my limit would be around £500 a month.

EA: Well, I've got a couple of things here that might suit you. There's a ground floor flat that's within walking distance of the university, in Edgbaston and a flat in Moseley which is on the, er, third floor.

JT: Sorry, did you say Moseley? How do you spell that?

EA: M-O-S-E-L-E-Y.

JT: Thanks. Is that far from the uni?

EA: No, not very far, and there's a direct bus there, which runs pretty frequently, I think. Moseley's a nice place to live, too.

JT: Are they furnished?

EA: The one in Moseley is fully furnished, but the other one isn't.

JT: How much are they?

EA: The one near the uni is £480 per calendar month.

JT: OK. And how much is the flat in Moseley?

EA: That's £520 a month.

JT: That's a bit more than I want to pay.

EA: I know, but it's a really nice flat. I think you should have a look at it.

JT: Does the rent include any bills?

EA: All of our properties have water rates included, but gas, electric and phone – they're your responsibility I'm afraid.

JT: OK. When can I view these places?

EA: When is convenient for you?

JT: I'm pretty flexible and I'd really like to find somewhere quite soon.

EA: How about this afternoon?

JT: Great.

EA: Why don't we meet at the Moseley flat, and have a look at that, and then we can go on to the other one afterwards.

JT: Good. So what's the address?

EA: Have you got a pen? Good. It's 375 Greenfield Road, that's G-R-E-E-N-F-I-E-L-D all one word, road and it's just off the High Street. Meet me outside the front door and I'll take you up to the third floor to see the flat.

JT: Fine.

EA: Have you got a mobile phone number, too in case anything goes wrong?

JT: Of course. It's 0791 357629.

EA: Sorry, did you say 619?

JT: No, 357629. Great. Well, I'll see you there at, um, would three o'clock be OK?

EA: Oh, I'm sorry, I've actually got an appointment with another client at three. Could we make it 4.15?

JT: Yes, that's fine.

EA: Good. 4.15, it is then, Mr …

JT: Taylor – John Taylor.

EA: I'll see you then.

Section 2

Good afternoon. It's good to see so many of you here. I hope that you're all settling down well here in Sydney. I'm here this afternoon to talk about one of Sydney's most famous assets – the beach! There are many beautiful beaches in the city, and you can have a lot of fun at them, but it's wise to be aware of a few things when you're there.

You've probably heard about shark attacks, but in fact, they're pretty rare. Usually it's surfers, who are quite far out in the water. It's true that there are about two or three attacks a year, but if you think about the number of people who swim on the coast, the chance of getting bitten is very small. Another marine hazard are box jellyfish which can give you a very nasty sting, but they're only really a problem further up the coast where the water is warmer, say from about Brisbane onwards.

Some of you, I know, are from climates much warmer than here, but for those of you who aren't, the sun is very strong here, especially in the summer months, and you should be really careful to slip-slap-slop, as we say here: slip on a shirt, slap on a hat and slop on some sun cream.

Finally, something that's much less well-known – rip currents in the ocean. You are far more likely to die in a rip current than any other way on the beach. What's a rip current, then? Well, if you are swimming in the sea and you suddenly notice that you are being pulled out to sea very fast, then you are probably in a rip current. It can be a terrifying experience – one minute you are swimming around quite happily, and the next, you are in the middle of a very strong current that is taking you away from the shore.

So what do you do? Well, most people panic and start trying to swim back towards the shore. This is the worst thing you can possibly do. You'll use up a lot of energy – and being in a panic will make the situation even worse – you'll become totally exhausted, and then it's far easier to drown. So that's the first message. Don't try to swim against it.

Secondly, don't panic. As long as you are relaxed, you'll conserve your energy. Usually, rips are quite narrow and run straight out, at right angles to the beach. So, instead of swimming towards the shore, swim parallel to it, across the current. This should take you out of the rip, and then you'll be able to come in to the shore. Sometimes, the current might be very strong, and you won't even be able to swim across it. However, the further you get away from the beach, the less power the current will have. When you feel the pull getting weaker, you can start swimming again, across the current, and you'll find that the waves will take you back to shore.

The best way to fight rip currents though is to follow a few basic rules. Never go swimming in the ocean alone, and if you're not a very strong swimmer, stick to shallow waters. Better still, only swim in places where there is a lifeguard. Enjoy the beach, and be safe.

Section 3

[A = Andrew, B = Balvir]

B: Hi Andrew. How's your new course going?
A: Biology? It's great – much better than Chemistry. I'm really glad I swapped.
B: What are you up to?
A: I'm trying to get prepared for the Biology presentations tomorrow.
B: Have you finished? I've got to do one for Business Studies, next week.
A: Well, sort of. I'm still struggling with which order to put things, but I know what I've got to say.
B: What's it about?
A: It took me ages to come up with a topic, but finally, I decided to look at an example of selective use of pesticides on crops.
B: Wow, that sounds impressive! What does it mean, exactly?

A: Well, you know that farmers use all sorts of chemicals on their crops, and a lot of them are for killing insects. A lot of the insects are a problem, they reduce yields and cause blemishes on the crops …
B: Like spots on apples, you mean?
A: Yes, exactly like that – or cotton is a good example. If it has any insects in it, or if they have damaged it, it's worth a fraction of what the farmer can get if it's perfect. It makes a huge difference to his profit margin. Of course, the down side to chemicals is that they're expensive, so that cuts into the farmer's profit too, but not as much.
B: So, the farmer wants to kill all the insects?
A: Yes, and no. In most cases, that's what happens. The farmer sprays an insecticide, a chemical that kills everything.
B: So what's the problem?
A: The problem is that some of the insects that are in the field are beneficial to the farmer – maybe they eat the harmful bugs, or maybe they help to pollinate the crop, or something like that.
B: Mm.
A: And so, the problem for the farmer is that they want to be able to kill insects selectively.
B: Is that possible?
A: It is, but it's difficult. I found this one example that I really liked, and that's what I want to talk about in my presentation. It's so clever.
B: OK, so tell me about it. You can practise for tomorrow.
A: Well, it's an example from a farmer with fruit trees. Think about the kind of insects that you don't want on fruit – all of the ones that crawl about – caterpillars, snails, that kind of thing.
B: Beetles?
A: No, usually they're OK. The ones that you do want all have wings – bees, wasps, butterflies, most beetles too.
B: Yeah, so how can you kill one lot and not the other?
A: This is where it's so clever. The farmer paints a ring of insecticide around the trunk of the tree.
B: But won't that kill everything?
A: Only any insects that touch it. Now the farmer sprays the tree with a natural pyrethrum.
B: A what?
A: Pyrethrum – it's a kind of insecticide made from flowers. It doesn't really kill insects, it just stuns them so that they fall out of the tree.
B: All of them?
A: Yes, all of them. Now the insects with wings – the good, useful insects – they will just fly back up to the tree afterwards, but the crawling insects will try to get up the tree trunk, and will come into contact with the other insecticide, and die.
B: Wow, that's clever. I think that that should work well for your presentation tomorrow.
A: I hope so. I'm going to talk a bit about insects becoming immune to insecticides too.
B: Well, good luck. I'm sure it'll be a really interesting talk.

Section 4

Last week we looked at the stock market and how it functions, and so, today, I want to go on to look at business ownership and corporations – what they are, and some reasons why they are formed.

I'd like to start by talking about two different types of business ownership. If you start a restaurant by taking your own money to buy the building and the equipment, then what you have done is formed a sole proprietorship. You own the entire restaurant yourself. You get to make all of the decisions and you keep all of the profit. If three people pool their money together and start a restaurant as a team, what they have done is formed a partnership. The three people own the restaurant themselves, sharing the profit and decision-making.

A rather different way of setting up a business is to become a corporation. Any business that wants to sell shares of stock to a number of different people does so by turning itself into a corporation. This is in all legal ways like a person, and it can act as an individual acts. It's registered with the government, it can own property, it can go to court to sue people, it can be sued and it can make contracts. By definition, a corporation has stock that can be bought and sold, and all of the owners of the corporation hold shares of stock to represent their ownership. So, for example, if I buy ten per cent of the shares of a certain corporation, then I have a one tenth ownership of the company.

There is a whole body of law that controls corporations – these laws are in place to protect the shareholders and the public. These laws control a number of things about how a corporation operates and is organized. For example, every corporation has a board of directors. It's unlikely, but even if all of the shares of a corporation are owned by one person, then that one person can decide that there will only be one person on the board of directors, but there is still a board. The shareholders in the company meet every year to vote on the people for the board. The board of directors makes the decisions for the company. It hires the officers of the company, for example, the president, makes the company's decisions

and sets the company's policies. The board of directors can be thought of as the brain of the company – they don't do any of the work of the company, but they make the important decisions.

Let's look at this flow chart of how a corporation works. Firstly, of course, a business idea has to be generated. It's often something that needs a lot of capital, and one of the big reasons why corporations exist is to create a structure for collecting lots of money for investment in a business. Let's say that you would like to start your own airline. Most people cannot do this, because an aeroplane costs millions of dollars. An airline needs a whole fleet of planes and other equipment, plus it has to hire a lot of employees. A person who wants to start an airline will therefore form a corporation and sell shares of stock in order to collect the money needed to get started. The company might sell one million shares of stock at $20 a share to raise $20 million very quickly. The company then invests the $20 million in equipment and employees. The investors (the shareholders who bought the $20 million in stock) hope that with the equipment and employees, the company will make a profit and pay a dividend.

Another reason that corporations exist is to limit the liability of the owners to some extent. If the corporation gets sued, it is the corporation that pays the settlement. The corporation may go out of business, but that is the worst that can happen. If you are a sole proprietor who owns a restaurant and the restaurant gets sued, you are the one who is being sued. You and the restaurant are the same thing. If you lose the suit then you, personally, can lose everything you own in the process, and this is obviously not desirable.

CD Track Listing

Track 1	Recording 1	Track 17	Recording 17
Track 2	Recording 2	Track 18	Recording 18
Track 3	Recording 3	Track 19	Recording 19
Track 4	Recording 4	Track 20	Recording 20
Track 5	Recording 5	Track 21	Recording 21
Track 6	Recording 6	Track 22	Recording 22
Track 7	Recording 7	Track 23	Recording 23
Track 8	Recording 8	Track 24	Recording 24
Track 9	Recording 9	Track 25	Recording 25
Track 10	Recording 10	Track 26	Recording 26
Track 11	Recording 11	Track 27	Recording 27
Track 12	Recording 12	Track 28	Practice Test Section 1
Track 13	Recording 13	Track 29	Practice Test Section 2
Track 14	Recording 14	Track 30	Practice Test Section 3
Track 15	Recording 15	Track 31	Practice Test Section 4
Track 16	Recording 16	Track 32	Copyright information